The Illustrated Guide to
Saddle Fitting

An Easy Visual Reference to
Ensure Health, Comfort, and
Performance for You and Your Horse

Beverly Harrison

TRAFALGAR SQUARE
North Pomfret, Vermont

First published in 2024 by
Trafalgar Square Books
North Pomfret, Vermont 05053

Disclaimer of Liability

The author and publisher shall have neither liability nor responsibility to any person or entity with respect to any loss or damage caused or alleged to be caused directly or indirectly by the information contained in this book. While the book is as accurate as the author can make it, there may be errors, omissions, and inaccuracies.

Trafalgar Square Books encourages the use of approved safety helmets in all equestrian sports and activities.

Trafalgar Square Books certifies that the content in this book was generated by a human expert on the subject, and the content was edited, fact-checked, and proofread by human publishing specialists with a lifetime of equestrian knowledge. TSB does not publish books generated by artificial intelligence (AI).

Library of Congress Cataloging-in-Publication Data

Names: Harrison, Beverly (Horse specialist), author.
Title: The illustrated guide to saddle fitting : an easy visual reference to ensure health, comfort,
   and performance for you and your horse / Beverly Harrison.
Description: North Pomfret : Trafalgar Square Books, 2024. | Includes index.
Identifiers: LCCN 2024022971 (print) | LCCN 2024022972 (ebook) | ISBN 9781646012541 (hardback) |
   ISBN 9781646012558 (epub)
Subjects: LCSH: English saddles--Fitting. | Western saddles--Fitting.
Classification: LCC SF309.9 .H373 2024 (print) | LCC SF309.9 (ebook) | DDC 636.1/0837--dc23/eng/20240711
LC record available at https://lccn.loc.gov/2024022971
LC ebook record available at https://lccn.loc.gov/2024022972 Original artwork by Beverly Harrison

Book design by Lauryl Eddlemon
Cover design by RM Didier
Index by Andrea Jones (JonesLiteraryServices.com)

Printed in China

10 9 8 7 6 5 4 3 2 1

To the horses,
who make us who we are

Contents

Preface

Those of us born with a passion for horses would be hard-pressed to explain it, but we certainly understand it and recognize it in each other. My best, lifelong friends are those I have met in a classroom or on the bus to work, and who are also horse lovers, and we instantly gravitated to each other. That fascination that we have makes us excited and endlessly curious about all things horse related.

In my case, I was touching, smelling, and sitting on horses before I could walk. Riding has been my therapy, means of mobility, and passion, but it has also posed dilemmas due to hip and knee deformities that I was born with. I was a "pretzel baby" with no hip joints and unformed knees that have required lifelong medical intervention, surgeries, therapy, and riding modifications. As is often the case, the thing that makes pursuing a goal difficult is the thing that pushes us harder to achieve it.

As a craftsman and an artist, I like to make things with my hands, so saddle repair, maintenance, and modification became a form of "functional art" for me. Combining my skills as a saddler (one who works on saddles) with my lifetime's worth of observational understanding of horses and what they tell us about their comfort or discomfort led me to a career in saddle fitting. Recognizing what horses express to us is the most powerful tool of all in pursuing an equestrian skill; saddle fitting is no exception.

In 1997, following a career in environmental science, I chose to start my own business, The Tack Collection, in Colorado. By that time, I had worked on tack and worked in tack stores since 1970, and I was dismayed by the lack of saddle selection and basic understanding of tack and its purpose. An encore profession followed, one that provided an opportunity to pursue my lifelong passion. I immediately realized my need for further education in order to support the express need for educated saddle fitting in opposition to the prevalent path of saddle sales. I found that nothing existed at that time within the United States to provide a thorough education in saddle fitting basics and protocol. It was through my friends in the English saddlery business in the United Kingdom that I discovered the Society of Master Saddlers (SMS). I became involved as an overseas member and participated in the first course in Saddle Fitting offered by SMS to Overseas Members in 1999. I have continued that membership, protocol, and continuing education, which all provided a framework for my profession and as I educate others. The information contained in this book is structured around that basic protocol and supplemented with information from courses in equine movement and physiology, saddlery design, and human mobility as equestrians.

I mentioned earlier that I am an artist—I'm a painter, a sculptor, and a creator of textile art. I think in visual terms first and then try to fit the visual concept into words. I have loved the process of writing this book because it opened the door to education in a personal way. I can literally *show you* what I am trying to say through the artwork in these pages. This is my first experience with illustration, so the images in this book are not polished in a way a professional illustrator would provide. They are "painterly," they are spontaneous, and they attempt to represent what I feel are the most important aspects of the information I'm trying to impart.

The skills of listening to and observing both horse and rider are key to piecing together saddle-fitting solutions. If our goal is to find a saddle that a particular horse works well in while addressing a rider's specific needs, we must have a procedure to work through the many variables that exist. Otherwise, we are gambling with the horse's welfare, the riders' ability to ride well, and a significant financial investment.

I personally have had horses that are difficult to fit, as well as physical riding challenges and limited resources. What has gotten me through all of that is to live with a philosophy of never giving up and never ceasing to learn. Persistence, patience, and curiosity are the attributes I strive to develop in my horsemanship and in my life. And the happiness and well-being of horses is my motivation, paramount to all else.

Bev Harrison
Lafayette, Colorado

Introduction

Saddles can be, and often are, a link to the horses we have put
them on. They are more than useful tools that we use in order to ride
effectively. They literally take on the shape of the rider and the horse,
imprinting the connection of the rider on the top and the horse on the bottom. When
passed on from someone else, a trainer or parent perhaps, that individual is imprinted
on the saddle as well. The care that we have taken of that saddle makes it more beau-
tiful over time. The excitement of purchasing a brand-new saddle, or a used saddle, for
equestrians, often surpasses the thrill of a new car, new clothes, or new boots. When we
hit frustrations in training or unsoundness in our horses, many times it is the saddle that
goes, in the hope a new saddle will solve the problem. There is mystique involved. There
is nostalgia involved. There is peer pressure involved—along with lots of other things that
affect our judgment.

This book's aim is to give you a way forward, with confidence, in evaluating saddle fit
and saddle safety; a cookbook, if you will. There will be a list of ingredients, an ordered
process, and a description of the finished product. Just like a cooking recipe, there are
endless variables that cannot be predicted. There are individual interpretations that will
result in unique results. With patience and care, you should end up with a decent loaf of
bread, or in this case, a saddle that will be helpful to both horse and rider. Will you be as
skilled as the equivalent chef that has baked tens of thousands loaves of bread? Of course
not! But you will be able to get by if you don't have help. And you will be able to distinguish

if a person you may have asked or hired to help you has the necessary understanding. You will have a greater appreciation of the process. Most importantly, you will have the tools to quickly know if your horse needs help with his saddle.

While the focus of this book is English-style saddles, many concepts in these pages will flow over to other types of saddles. There is information that is presented to help you understand your horse and your horse's movement, as well as to highlight the importance of the rider's position. Many facets of information must come together in order to have the positive result our horses deserve.

Does it take a trained saddle fitter with years of experience to evaluate the fit of a saddle for a horse and rider? Sometimes it is absolutely necessary, and it is *always* going to be an advantage if you have such advice available to you. *Does it take a degree in engineering to sort through all the complicated variables involved in selecting a saddle?* Seldom, although it does help to sort through the issues logically. *Can a salesperson with a week of training and an assortment of saddles find the right saddle?* Maybe…but probably unlikely that an individual with minimal training will be able to find the right saddle for you and your horse.

It is you, the reader, the horse owner, the rider, who must have the control to safeguard your horse's comfort and safety when evaluating a saddle. Equally important to that initial evaluation is having the knowledge of awareness to keep horse and rider safe and effective in the saddle over time.

Who Is This Book For?

For the instructor who looks at many horses and riders with different kinds of tack, this book can help determine if a saddle is helping or hindering a horse's training process. Quite often, behavioral issues and training problems arise from ill-fitting tack, especially due to poor saddle fit or faulty saddle maintenance.

For the rider with a new horse, this information helps you to evaluate available saddles so that you can start enjoying your new equine partner. The aim of this book is to give an owner or rider the skills of self-sufficiency. When an owner takes charge of their horse's care with the support of valid information, everyone wins, particularly the horse. Advice on saddle fitting seems to come from many sources: sometimes it's the trainer, sometimes the barn owner, and sometimes from others at the barn who have advice and opinions on saddle fit, although they likely have little or no training on the subject. It is truly up to the owner to filter the accuracy of information sources.

For the medical practitioner, this book helps to pinpoint reoccurring problems that may be caused or aggravated by a saddle. No matter how comprehensive a university's veterinary curriculum is or how thorough alternative medicine training might be, in those educational venues, saddle fit cannot be given the time it requires for a complete understanding.

For riders and trainers with developing, injured, or aging horses, this information will provide a ready checklist to maintain your equine partner's health and comfort. A well-fitting saddle helps that horse to develop in a positive way. Horses change shape surprisingly quickly as they progress in training, as the training changes, as their rehabilitation proceeds, and as their bodies mature. Saddle evaluation must coincide with that inevitable change.

As you read on, you will find:

❋ A guide to terminology so that we are all speaking the same language.

❋ The basics of saddle construction so that you know what you are looking at and feeling.

❋ Useful information about horse and rider anatomy that is key to the saddle fitting process.

✳ Important safety issues to keep avoidable accidents in check.

✳ A saddle fit checklist for the horse standing still, a checklist for the rider on the horse's back, and a checklist for the ridden horse. These are intended to be quick refreshers and reminders as time goes on.

✳ Clues as to what affects the fit of your saddle.

✳ How to determine when your saddle needs maintenance.

So, let's get started!

Parts and Styles of the English Saddle

Terminology and Saddle Construction

Terminology for saddle components is fairly standard, but there can be some ambiguity because of individual manufacturers' preferences or terms from the Western saddle world assumed to apply to English saddles, as well. For example, to some a *gullet* is a part of the saddle that fits over the horse's withers, but technically it is the midline of the underside of the saddle that protects the horse's spine.

This chapter will lay the groundwork for how we can precisely communicate about a saddle. This is easiest with illustrations—my favorite way to explain things.

The top of the saddle (meaning the top surface, whether from the actual top or the side) is the view to which we are most accustomed. The different parts of the saddle are laid out in **Illustration 2.1 Saddle Surface Parts**. There, the parts of the top (seen from the side) and bottom of the saddle are identified for your convenient reference as you work through this book.

Additional Notes for Your Consideration

It is helpful to use the Illustrations in this section to identify parts of your own saddle. When you can name the areas that you can touch and are familiar with on a saddle, it clarifies how

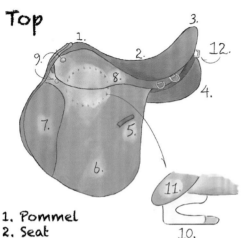

Top

Bottom

1. Pommel
2. Seat
3. Cantle
4. Panel
5. Stirrup Leather Keeper
6. Flap
7. Knee Roll
8. Skirt
9. Nail Head
10. Stirrup Bar
11. Point Pocket
12. Crupper Bar (optional)

1. Gullet
2. Panel
3. Sweat Flap
4. Billet
5. Flap
6. Crupper Bar (optional)

each segment is designed to provide stability and comfort to both the horse and the rider. The *material* the saddle is made of, the kind of *tree* that is used for the saddle, and the kind of *panel* that is used are parts that have lots of variability and options. Those options are briefly discussed in this section (other parts are identified, as well, for your information).

Material Details

Often, the English saddle is constructed from leather of different varieties, although synthetic material is also used. The leather must be maintained correctly through regular cleaning and conditioning, and is more expensive to produce while synthetic materials require no real maintenance and are less expensive for the manufacturer. Both hold up well if adequately cared for.

Tree Details

The *tree* of a saddle functions much like the skeleton in our bodies (**Illustration 2.2 Tree Anatomy)**. It is critical to the stability and fit of the saddle. The concept of a tree is often misunderstood because the majority of riders haven't seen a saddle stripped down to the tree. Visualization of this fundamental structure is useful as we address the correct fit elements later in the book.

The tree can be made of *wood* or of *synthetic* material. Wooden trees in all but the cheapest saddles have a steel *head plate* (also sometimes called a *gullet plate*) and steel *bands*, slightly thinner than a steel ruler, that run from the front to the back of the saddle. They instill strength and stability while still allowing controlled flexibility through the tree to accommodate the horse's movement. Steel components are secured to wooden trees with steel rivets. (Rivets function similarly to nails or screws but are short with blunt ends.)

Routine safety checks are important to ensure the integrity of the saddle that is dependent on the integrity of the tree. Wood spring trees can break, come loose, or twist. Synthetic trees can crack, break, or twist.

Wood Spring

1. Head
2. Gullet Plate with Rivets
3. Point
4. Stirrup Bar
5. Rail of Tree
6. Steel Spring
7. Waist or Twist
8. Cantle
9. Width of Tree
Measurement, cm

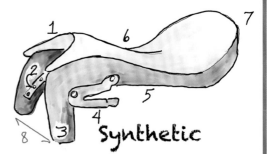

Synthetic

1. Head
2. Steel Gullet Plate
3. Point of Tree
4. Stirrup Bar
5. Rail of Tree
6. Waist or Twist
7. Cantle
8. Width of Tree
Measurement, cm

Notice that the *stirrup bars* (**see both Illustrations 2.1 and 2.2**) are riveted to the tree for strength and stability. The *billets,* which, by virtue of the girth, keep the saddle on the horse, are critical to rider safety and therefore attached to the tree either by sewing the billets to webbing that runs over the top of the tree before the seat is placed on, or by securing the webbing directly to the tree. Foam padding is placed over the tree for rider comfort, then the seat, skirt, and flaps are added to the top side. The *panels* (see more about these below) are stitched onto the bottom portion of the tree by hand, sometimes reinforced with screws. The stitching is "hidden," and a lacing type of stitch is used with very strong saddler's thread to keep the panel lined up with the tree. It is important that great care is taken throughout the manufacturing process to keep the saddle symmetrical.

> *Care must be taken during the manufacturing process to ensure saddle symmetry.*

Panel Details

The *panel* of an English saddle, which you can see in both the side and bottom view of **Illustration 2.1**, is in contact with the back of the horse and padded in some fashion. (This is unlike a Western saddle that has only sheepskin stitched on the "horse side" of the saddle. Padding is provided through blankets and pads.) The English panel is designed to address the need for compression required to absorb force from the weight of the rider. Inside the panel, which is essentially a leather envelope, is *wool flocking* (sheep's wool, processed specifically for the English saddle), synthetic flocking (usually Dacron®, a polyester fiber, specific for insertion into the English panel), foam rubber (generally a closed cell foam that holds its shape), or a combination of these. In some instances, air bladders are used as the padding. There are advantages and disadvantages for each of these options, and it is important to realize that *all* of these padding materials can deform and require maintenance or replacement.

Styles of English Saddles for Different Riding Disciplines

Thinking of different riding disciplines stimulates a visual image to those of us who have participated in the English riding world. Cross-country jumping is a very different image than competitive dressage or polo. Saddles designed for those specific purposes look quite different from each other because of the objectives of the specific discipline, yet they are all fit to the horse and rider using the same methods explained in this book. Recognizing the style differences allows the rider to choose the best type of saddle for their intended use.

Illustration 2.3 Style Comparison is useful for making the comparisons explained in descriptions that follow.

✳ An image of *dressage* riding evokes a controlled balance between horse and rider as they move in increasingly complex ways while they advance in training. Originally, the term dressage simply meant "classical training" from which a horse was better able to jump or maneuver on uneven terrain while understanding the rider's requests. In general, the rider stays seated with lengthened legs and the body upright over the center of balance of the horse.

✳ A *jumping, hunt seat, or close contact* style saddle is designed for maximizing rider position while navigating obstacles, though some riders prefer this style on the flat, as well. The rider has a shortened stirrup that allows for an angle at the hip, knee, and ankle. There is a corresponding angle to the rider's upper body as it hinges at the waist to assist the horse's balance over jumps or when galloping. Usually the saddle's seat is more shallow than a dressage saddle because, while the rider may be in a sitting position part of the time, it is important for the rider to balance on her feet to rise to a *half-seat* or *two-point position*. This transfers the rider's weight over the leg rather than in the saddle's seat. With increased height of the jumps, the flaps of the saddle become

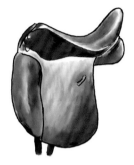

Dressage

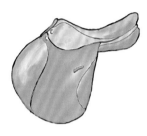

Jump or Hunt Seat

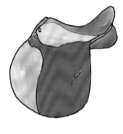

General Purpose

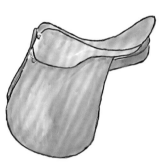

Polo

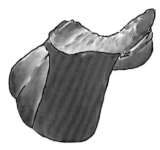

Trekking or Trail

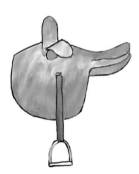

Side Saddle

more angled to accommodate a shorter stirrup requirement. Some jumping saddles are specifically designed for *cross-country riding* by deepening the seat slightly and providing larger knee rolls to assist a rider traveling over uneven terrain and over a variety of jumps at speed.

✳ Should a rider wish to participate in both dressage and jumping with one saddle, or for a rider who is interested in general pleasure riding, she may choose a *general purpose* saddle. This style encompasses a deeper seat and also a larger leg flap, allowing for lengthening or shortening of the rider's leg in the stirrups as needed. While useful as an all-around saddle because of its versatility, this style may be limiting when the rider chooses to pursue more serious dressage or jumping efforts. A deeper seat makes it harder to rise from the seat over jumps, and the leg flaps make it more difficult to maintain a classically upright dressage position.

✳ *Polo* saddles are designed for use on the flat at speed, involving fast changes in direction, and are built to suit a long leg position set slightly more forward than the previously described styles. This facilitates more maneuverability in the saddle across the polo field. The seat is flatter and more open to allow a rider to move the torso forward or back, or to twist and swing to strike the polo ball. A thinner panel enables a polo rider to stay close to the horse's back, which increases a rider's maneuverability. Polo saddles are also lightweight but sturdy.

✳ *Trekking, endurance,* and *long distance* saddles tend to have a more padded seat for the rider. The seat is often quilted to encourage circulation in the upper legs and buttocks as a rider sits for prolonged periods of time. The panels tend to be more padded for the horse and are often wider to provide a greater bearing surface on the horse's back, distributing the weight of the rider and gear over the back in a way to reduce the pounds per square inch. (The rules of physics come into play: increasing surface area reduces the pounds per square inch, thus distributing the pressure.) The knee rolls are well padded to avoid chafing the rider. These saddles also have more rings and hooks attached to the area surrounding the seat and on which a rider can hang gear helpful to support longer rides. *Crupper bars* in the very back of the cantle are often added to these saddles. This is a piece of hardware that is generally screwed into the back of the cantle, allowing a crupper strap to slide through. The crupper strap, generally made of leather, is placed around the dock of the horse's tail to keep the saddle from sliding forward when traveling on steep terrain. The piece around the dock of the horse's tail is specially designed to conform comfortably and avoid chaffing.

* *Side saddles*, once the mandatory saddle for female riders who were not encouraged to "ride astride," are still in use for competition, exhibition, and pleasure. The rider, generally wearing a long full skirt, is seated in the middle of the seat of the saddle (usually flat front to back) with the hips directed to the left side of the horse. The basic construction of the saddle is most similar to a dressage saddle, but there is a flap only on the left side. Both of the rider's legs sit to the left side, with a stirrup provided for the rider's left leg, while the right leg wraps over a horn. There may or may not be a stirrup for the right leg.

3

Basic Anatomy and Physiology of the Horse as It Relates to the Saddle

In this chapter, we touch on anatomy to further our conversation about saddle fit with greater precision. Incorrect assumptions concerning the meaning of terms, especially anatomical terms, may cause confusion and halt progress in improving the health and performance of the horse.

The Skeleton

Illustration 3.1 Horse under Saddle with Rider, Skeletal Components gives us a visual image to begin our conversation. When looking at how the human skeleton is seated on the horse's skeleton in the classically correct position (with ear, shoulder, hip, and heel aligned—as noted by the red vertical line), notice the human is over the horse's center of balance in a location where the horse's back can bear weight and still allow the shoulder to move (more on the importance of this later—see p. 56).

To be "on the same page" when talking about saddle fitting, we need to understand simplified equine structure (*anatomy*) and also equine function (*physiology*). **Illustration 3.2 Regional Anatomy of the Horse** provides the standard terminology we will use for regions of the horse in this book. In my travels, fitting saddles in different regions of North America and in different barns, I have noticed a huge amount of variation in terminology

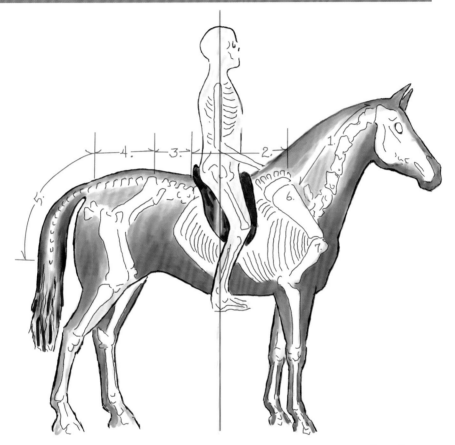

1. 7 Cervical Vertebrae,
2. 18 Thoracic Vertebrae
3. 6 Lumbar Vertebrae
4. 5 Sacral Vertebrae

5. 18-22 Coccygeal Vertebrae
6. Scapula
7. Humerus

used to describe parts of the horse. When referring to different areas on the horse, we tend to use the term we have heard most often, whether it is accurate or not. This illustration is intended to help avoid future confusion.

The horse's skeleton (*bony anatomy*) is critical to our understanding of how he moves and propels himself in locomotion, but it is even more crucial to consider the functional skeleton under the weight and influence of a rider. The saddle, when fitted in an optimal way, protects the bony structures and allows for unencumbered movement. The basics of the equine skeleton are laid out in **Illustration 3.3 Skeleton of the Horse, Side** and **Illustration 3.4 Skeleton of the Horse, Top**. Pay particular attention to the length of the

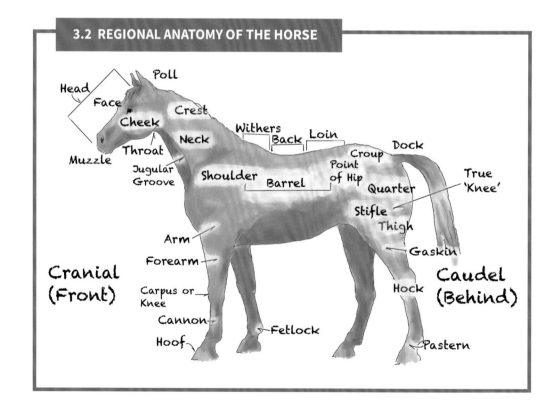

3.2 REGIONAL ANATOMY OF THE HORSE

3.3 SKELETON OF THE HORSE, SIDE

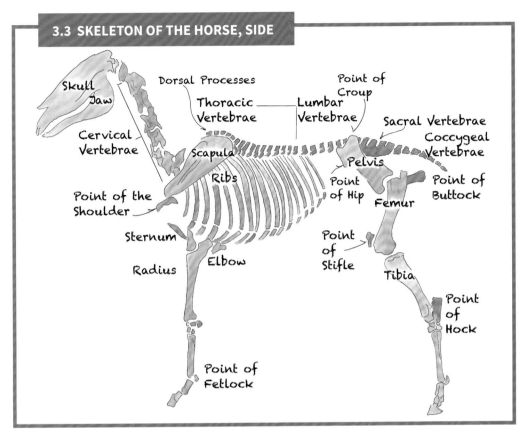

Skull
Jaw
Dorsal Processes
Thoracic Vertebrae
Lumbar Vertebrae
Point of Croup
Sacral Vertebrae
Coccygeal Vertebrae
Cervical Vertebrae
Scapula
Pelvis
Point of Hip
Point of Buttock
Ribs
Femur
Point of the Shoulder
Sternum
Point of Stifle
Radius
Elbow
Tibia
Point of Hock
Point of Fetlock

3.4 SKELETON OF THE HORSE, TOP

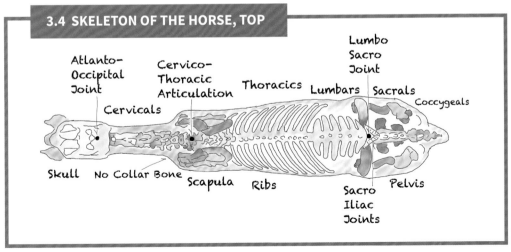

Atlanto-Occipital Joint
Cervico-Thoracic Articulation
Thoracics
Lumbars
Sacrals
Lumbo Sacro Joint
Coccygeals
Cervicals
Skull
No Collar Bone
Scapula
Ribs
Sacro Iliac Joints
Pelvis

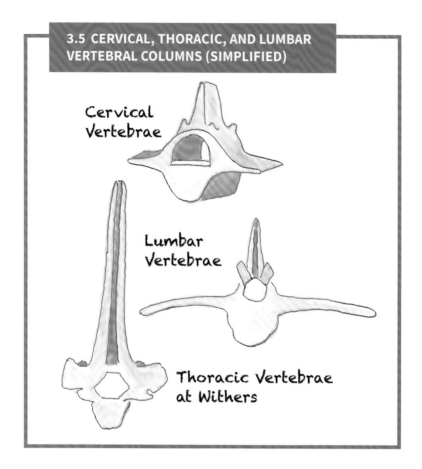

3.5 CERVICAL, THORACIC, AND LUMBAR VERTEBRAL COLUMNS (SIMPLIFIED)

Cervical Vertebrae

Lumbar Vertebrae

Thoracic Vertebrae at Withers

thoracic region of the spine and the orientation of the *ribs*. A closeup of the spinal segments is shown in **Illustration 3.5 Cervical, Thoracic, and Lumbar Vertebral Columns (Simplified)**. It is important to understand and visualize their shape and orientation when we later discuss how to determine the appropriate length of an English saddle (see p. 66).

Paramount to understanding the importance of protecting the spine when fitting a saddle is recognition of areas where there is less separation or space between the top of the spinous process between the vertebrae. Interference of one spinous process with another is referred to as *kissing spines* and demonstrated in **Illustration 3.6 Kissing Spines**.

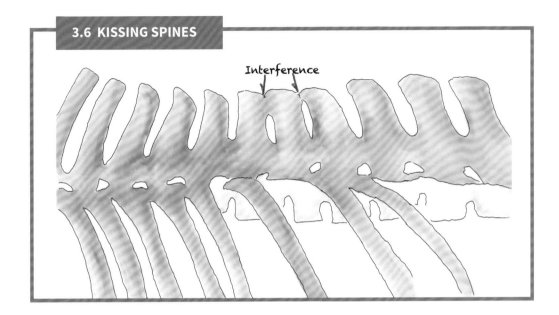

3.6 KISSING SPINES

Interference

Visualizing this potential malfunction of the spine is helpful as we focus on ways to keep the horse's back strong and pain-free.

Ligaments, coupled with developed abdominal muscles, provide support and mobility to the horse's spine. Pain from many sources, but from the saddle, in particular, causes a horse to "drop" his back in an effort to pull away from the origin of discomfort, thereby reducing the space between the top of the spinous processes and potentially leading to impingement. In contrast, a strong, elastic, and pain-free back "lifts" toward the saddle, opening the space between the vertebrae, in a way similar to what happens when a horse lowers his neck to graze (**Illustration 3.7 Mechanics of Lifting and Dropping the Equine Back**). Any compromise of the space and orientation of the spinal column has a direct effect on the *nerve bundles* that run through the spinal column to connect the horse's brain to the *spinal cord*. Notice in **Illustration 3.8 Spinal Cord and Nerve Bundles** how the nerves connect at their roots to the spinal cord and exit through the spinal column. The nerves that extend throughout a horse's body, and in particular, to the limbs, tell the horse where he is

Nuchal Ligament

Supraspinous Ligament

Separating Thoracic Spinous Processes
Nuchal Ligament Under Tension

Thoracic Spinous Process Comes Together
Nuchal Ligament Relaxed

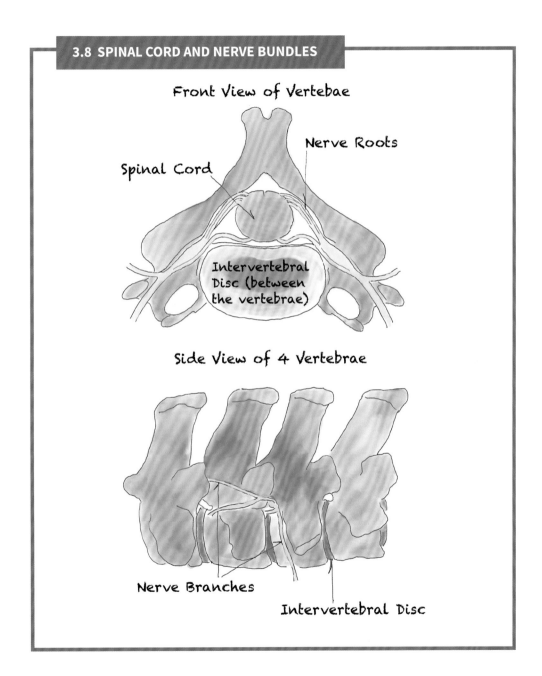

Front View of Vertebae

Nerve Roots

Spinal Cord

Intervertebral Disc (between the vertebrae)

Side View of 4 Vertebrae

Nerve Branches

Intervertebral Disc

in space. This is called *proprioception*. When nerves are constricted, pinched, or blocked, whether from poor spinal position or from direct pressure caused by an ill-fitting saddle, the horse's proprioception may be compromised, and correct movement may be painful or even impossible.

When the short, deep, *multifidus muscles* (which lie under the very long *longissimus dorsi muscle)* are weak and ineffective at stabilizing the spine, the horse will experience pain and fatigue. **Illustration 3.9 Deep Muscles to Stabilize the Spine** shows you how the vertebral column is linked together by these powerful muscles that work to keep the spine lined

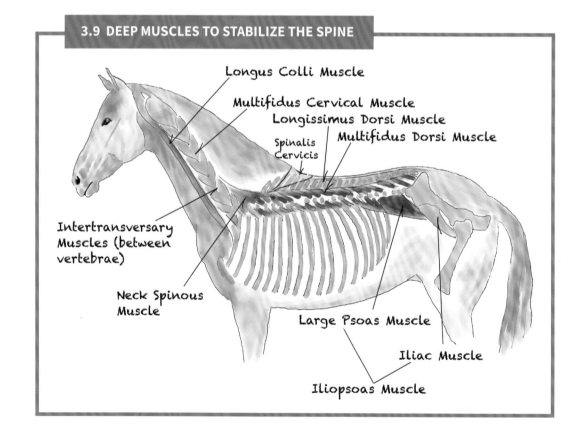

3.9 DEEP MUSCLES TO STABILIZE THE SPINE

Longus Colli Muscle

Multifidus Cervical Muscle

Longissimus Dorsi Muscle

Spinalis Cervicis

Multifidus Dorsi Muscle

Intertransversary Muscles (between vertebrae)

Neck Spinous Muscle

Large Psoas Muscle

Iliac Muscle

Iliopsoas Muscle

up in multiple directions. (Note: the complete muscles are not shown in the illustration due to layering, but general areas are indicated.) Even when only a portion of this muscle group is weak or damaged it is likely to affect other areas of the spine. (Current medical research shows very positive results in the individual's comfort and strength through rehabilitation that focuses on strengthening the *multifidus muscles*, in both horses and in humans.)

Superficial Muscle Groups

As we take a look at the horse's *superficial muscle groups*, the groups of muscles closest to the skin, consider the following questions:

✳ Can you picture the particular muscle groups I name on your own horse?

✳ Can you visualize what muscle groups your saddle sits on?

✳ How does a horse's shape change when moving under saddle? How does it change in shape from a "warm-up frame" to a "collected frame"? How does your saddle accommodate those postural changes? Or not?

✳ How does pressure (from the saddle, for example) potentially affect muscle development?

✳ What is *muscle atrophy* and how do we detect it?

Now take a look at **Illustration 3.10 Superficial Muscle Groups**. A fun project is to use chalk on a patient horse (a pile of tasty hay can help ensure this) and draw out a few of these muscle groups on his body. Then place your saddle on the horse's back *without* a saddle pad, and tighten the girth just enough to stabilize the saddle. Notice the position of the saddle and girth and ask yourself:

How might that addition of tack impact the muscles below?

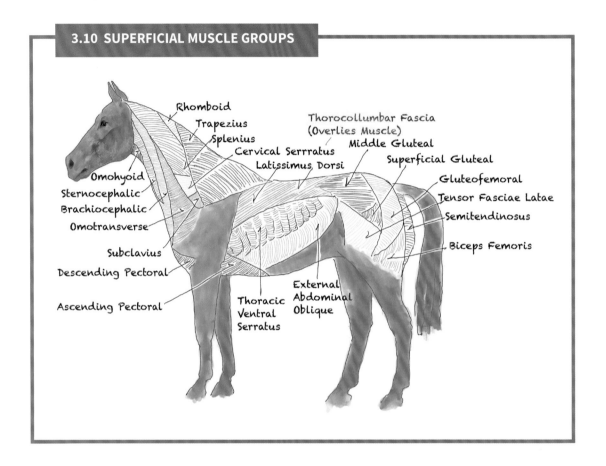

Rhomboid
Trapezius
Splenius
Cervical Serrratus
Latissimus Dorsi
Thorocollumbar Fascia
(Overlies Muscle)
Middle Gluteal
Superficial Gluteal
Gluteofemoral
Tensor Fasciae Latae
Semitendinosus
Biceps Femoris
Omohyoid
Sternocephalic
Brachiocephalic
Omotransverse
Subclavius
Descending Pectoral
Ascending Pectoral
Thoracic Ventral Serratus
External Abdominal Oblique

Conformation and Condition

Think about the different conformation shapes of a variety of horses: a racing Thorough-bred, a heavy draft horse, and a Quarter Horse, for example. These are well recognized as "types" of horses with a particular "shape" to their conformation, which will affect the size and style of saddle that will fit them best. Keep in mind that conformation is fixed, but fitness and body condition (that superficial muscle shape we just talked about, along with body fat) are variable. That is why professional saddle fitters use the same numerical scale for condition scoring that veterinarians do, as body condition drastically affects the fit of the saddle.

The following is the scoring system most commonly used by veterinarians and saddle fitters in the United States:

✳ Score 1: Emaciated. Bones of the spinous processes, ribs, tail-head, tuber coxae, and ischia all very prominent. Bone structure of neck, withers, and shoulders easily visible. No fat palpable over lumbar vertebral transverse processes.

✳ Score 2: Very thin. Bones of the spinous processes slightly rounded but visible. Ribs, tail head, tuber coxae and tuber ischia are prominent. Bone structure of neck, withers, and shoulders faintly discernible.

✳ Score 3: Thin. Some fat buildup halfway on spinous processes in loins and tail head, but both are prominent. Individual vertebrae in neck are not visible but can be easily felt. Slight fat buildup over ribs and tuber coxae but still easily visible.

✳ Score 4: Lean. Slight bony ridge over loins or flat, faint outline of ribs visible. Tail head prominence depending on breed, but fat should be palpable. Tuber coxae bones not easily visible. Withers, shoulder, and neck not obviously thin.

✳ Score 5: Moderate. Loins are flat (no crease or ridge). Ribs not easily visible but easily felt. Fat around tail-head is spongy, withers somewhat rounded (depending on breed). Shoulders and neck blend smoothly into body.

✳ Score 6: Moderately fleshy. May have slight crease down loins, ribs palpable with light pressure, and fat around tail-head is soft. Some fat palpable on side of withers, neck, and behind shoulder.

* Score 7: Fleshy. May have crease down loins, and ribs difficult to feel. Palpable fat deposited along withers, behind shoulder, and along neck.

* Score 8: Fat. Negative crease down loins. Ribs very difficult to feel, and fat around tail head very soft. Fat filling area over withers and behind shoulder with noticeable thickening of neck.

* Score 9: Obese. Obvious crease down loins. Fat bulging around tail-head, along withers, behind shoulders, and along neck. Flank filled with fat (no abdominal tuck and ribs hard to palpate).

The assignment of a body condition score informs a temporary saddle fit. As the horse's condition evolves, both in weight and musculature, fit needs to be reevaluated. The saddle sits on an area of fat and muscle along the horse's back. If we fit a horse with a body condition score of "5" when the horse is in significant work, then come back in six months after the horse has been on pasture with very light work and now displaying a body score of "7" (for example), the saddle is no longer going to fit. With this in mind, it is helpful to the horse and to the fit of the saddle if the owner keeps the horse at a reasonably consistent body condition score. (Note that horses scoring at the extremes of the scale on either end are not in a condition where riding, with or without a saddle, is recommended.)

Anatomy and Physiology of the Rider as It Relates to the Saddle

For successful saddle fitting, it is as important to address the dynamic stability of the rider as it is the horse. A horse should be able to perform at his best without discomfort. The same is true for a rider.

Common Challenges for Riders

Some elements make it more challenging when evaluating a rider's fit in the saddle in any English discipline, whether it is dressage, jumping, trail riding, or another activity. The following are just a few tricky issues that saddle fitters run across:

＊ There is often a mismatch between a rider's perception and reality because human cognitive sensory information relies on patterns. As an example, if a rider regularly sits to the right side of the horse whenever mounted, the brain believes this position is correct and straight. In brief, the rider's perception of her position and actions in the saddle is frequently inaccurate! As a result of this perception, when asked what kind of saddle fit a rider "likes," the rider will usually "like what she knows," versus "knowing what she likes." We humans like familiarity, even when it is damaging.

* A rider may believe her horse's lameness or movement issue is due to a problem with the horse, even though the horse doesn't appear lame until the rider mounts up. Rider-influenced causes tend to go unnoticed, and instead we focus on the horse when we *should* be addressing the *rider's* issues, or a problem with the fit of the equipment used.

* Riders, particularly more advanced riders, regularly ride through physical pain. That pain causes distortion of their position and compensatory movement. Rider compensations, often enacted unconsciously, occur to maximize the rider's own comfort and effectiveness, but they typically affect the movement of the horse in a detrimental way.

* There is not much consistency in the education of riders today, particularly in the United States, where a standardized curriculum does not exist. Theories and techniques are mostly up to individual trainers, with little commonality between trainers, and we do not have a precise standardized terminology with which to teach riders.

* Amateur riders generally spend most of their time in *non*-riding activities. Many of those activities undermine the symmetry that is so important to riding. For example, static positions assumed while driving a car or sitting at a computer all day create stiffness and asymmetry in the body, and weakness of the core muscles. It is clear that horses develop a locomotor strategy to compensate for such inconsistency and rigidity in the rider. The outcome of rider asymmetry, such as significantly weighting one stirrup more than the other, pulling on one rein (thus using one seat bone more than the other), or collapsing through one side all causes the saddle to compress more on the weighted side and shift to the weighted side compromising the horse's spine, and can deform the shape of the panels, as well as cause compensatory movement in the horse.

All the rider considerations just listed come into play when addressing saddle fit. *Ground reaction force (GRF)* from the horse's hooves contacting the ground come up through his limbs while the pressure of the rider pushes downward on the horse's back. The saddle sits in the middle. Consider a right-hand-dominant rider—that rider is likely stronger throughout her right side. In response, her horse may then brace through his ribcage on the right side, causing the saddle to collapse and deform on that side, or push sideways and shift more to the left. Either way, the result is crooked.

The amount of pressure from the rider on the horse's back increases with speed of locomotion:

* **Walk:** Pressure is equal to the weight of the rider.

* **Trot:** Pressure is two to three times the weight of the rider.

* **Canter:** Pressure is three to four times the weight of the rider.

With these numbers in mind, it is clear that at the walk, a crooked rider has less negative impact on a horse's back than at the trot and canter. Forces from the rider are increased in those faster gaits, as well as when jumping. The more suspension the horse has—the more bounce in the gaits—the greater the pressure from the rider. And it is also increased when the rider is stiff, unbalanced, or uncoordinated.

Rider Analysis for Today's Horses and Saddles

As equine athleticism increases through selective breeding, effective and balanced riding is much more challenging. It follows that there must be a change in the style of modern saddles to address the needs of the rider. As little as 30 to 40 years ago, jumping, dressage, and English-style trail saddles were essentially flat in the seat with very little, if any, knee roll. Now, saddles tend to have a deeper seat, larger knee rolls, sticky leather, and everything but a seat belt to keep riders more secure. This is particularly influenced by the number of amateur riders entering the market with a healthy budget for saddles with attributes that will help them achieve their goals on expensive, athletic horses.

When the seat of the saddle becomes deeper, with defined spots for the seat bones and knee rolls that control rider leg position, it is very easy to damage the rider if the saddle is not fit correctly—to both her and her horse. Anatomical features of each rider have to be recognized and understood when choosing a new saddle, or when achieving and maintaining balance in an existing saddle. I like to break down my analysis into different parts of the human body to identify problems: first, the rider's seat, then the trunk, and finally, the limbs.

Rider's Seat

The rider's seat is critical to both riding performance and comfort. How the rider sits determines her ability to give precise and symmetrical signals or aids via changes in her pelvic kinematics and weight distribution. The rider's pelvic alignment is simplified in **Illustration 4.1 Rider's Pelvic Alignment, Side View**. A pelvis in a *neutral position* is able to swing to the front (*anterior tilt*) and back (*posterior tilt*) in precise and measured ways. In an ideal rider-saddle-horse situation, the rider has a natural neutral pelvic alignment, the horse is naturally balanced with level posture (not structurally built "uphill" with the withers higher than the croup or "downhill" with the croup higher than the withers), and the saddle is fit in such a way as to put the rider's pelvis over the center of balance of the horse (see **Illustration 3.1**, p. 15), with the stirrup bars at the correct distance from the center of balance, and knee rolls that won't interfere with the rider's position.

A rider who sits predominantly in either *posterior tilt* or *anterior tilt* requires focused help. It is helpful to observe the posture of such a rider when she is *off* the horse. This first step is so important! It tells a saddle fitter or trainer how best to proceed in balancing the rider *on* the horse. For instance, if a rider has scoliosis, or a pelvic or spinal deformation, whether congenital or through injury, it must be understood that her "abnormal" joint position cannot be changed. Many riders are unaware of their structural issues except to notice

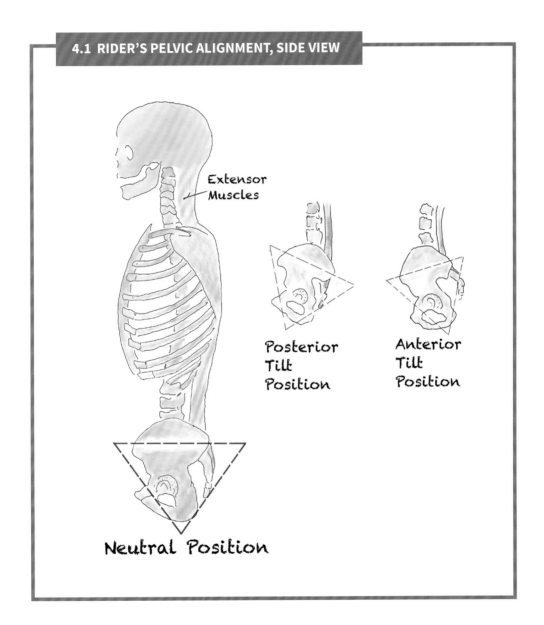

Extensor Muscles

Posterior Tilt Position

Anterior Tilt Position

Neutral Position

they are frequently sore in the back or hips after riding. A rider's muscles may be modified, although not quickly or easily. Instead, many times, the balance of a saddle needs adjustment for a particular rider to allow a more normal pelvic position and for better movement in the saddle. (Note: Such modifications require a very skilled saddler to make adjustments in a way that does not compromise saddle fit for the horse.)

A rider with a neutral pelvic position on the ground but a posterior tilt on the horse may be responding to a horse that has an "uphill" conformation; the reverse may be true for a rider with a neutral pelvic position on the ground but an anterior tilt on the horse due to "downhill" conformation. This assumes, however, that the saddle fit is correct for the horse. Now, let's consider the possibility that the saddle is *not* correct for the horse. What happens when the saddle slips forward during the ride over the scapula? Or, what about a saddle that is too narrow for the horse? In both cases, we see a rider with a posterior tilt. For a rider with a neutral pelvic position when unmounted but who sits with an anterior tilt in the saddle, the cause may be related to a saddle being too wide for the horse or the saddle's flocking may have collapsed in the front, making the saddle out of balance. It is also possible that the saddle has too much *gusset* (depth of panel) at the back of the saddle for the horse.

A rider in anything other than a neutral pelvic position may experience intense lower back pain that can damage her lumbar vertebrae, cause sacro-iliac misalignment, or result in nerve damage. And as already mentioned, the crooked or compensating rider causes a horse to move incorrectly, and this can elicit damage to a horse's joints, spine, and soft tissue.

Rider Structural Issues

In issues of rider scoliosis, or riders, such as myself, with hip and coinciding low back deformities, the problem solving when it comes to saddle fit and impact of rider structure on the horse becomes even more complex. **Illustration 4.2 Rider's Pelvic Alignment, Lateral Tilt** shows how the lifting and rotation of one seat bone deforms the rider's hip, leg, spine, and

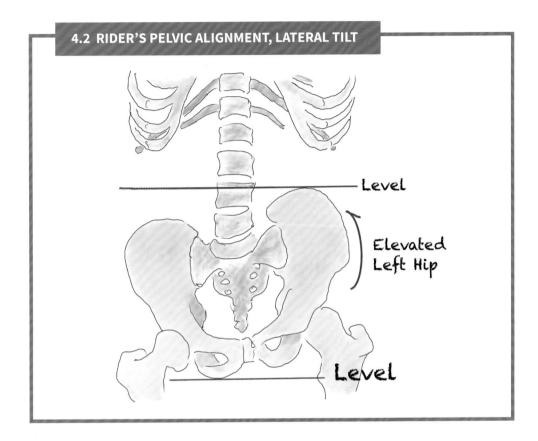

4.2 RIDER'S PELVIC ALIGNMENT, LATERAL TILT

Level

Elevated Left Hip

Level

even the shoulders and neck. I would like to say that this illustration is an exaggeration, but it is not.

Male vs. Female

For yet another variable, the female and male human pelvis is different, as shown in **Illustration 4.3, Comparison of Female and Male Pelvis**. One generalization that we can make with respect to gender is the width between the seat bones is greater in the female than the male. There are also significant individual variations of structure within the same human gender. It is not as simple as choosing a saddle "designed for a male" or "designed

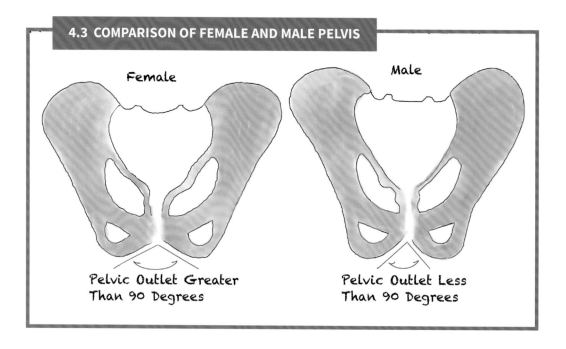

4.3 COMPARISON OF FEMALE AND MALE PELVIS

Female

Male

Pelvic Outlet Greater
Than 90 Degrees

Pelvic Outlet Less
Than 90 Degrees

for a female." Each individual must be considered carefully and allowed to try saddles with different *width of seat*, *width of twist* (or *waist*—see **Illustration 2.2**, p. 8), and *depth of seat* to accommodate their particular pelvic structure.

✳ A saddle *seat that is too wide* for a rider's seat bones makes it ambiguous for the rider to locate the center of the saddle. Discomfort is likely as the rider subconsciously moves from side to side, trying to balance over the center of the horse (while the horse grows confused, unsure of what the rider wants). When the *seat is too narrow*, the rider's seat bones fall to the outside of the seat support, and this can certainly elicit pain in the seat bones.

✳ In my experience fitting saddles, I have found that many females have an inward rotation of the hip from the pelvis, causing a tendency to "pinch" with the knee, particularly if the *twist of the saddle is too wide*. A twist that is too wide for the rider prohibits the rider's leg from relaxing into the correct position. A *twist that is too narrow* for the rider's pelvis means too much pressure will be on the pubic bone at the front of the pelvis, spelling pain!

✳ Depth of seat is commonly a matter of choice for the rider, but the pelvis of the individual must have enough room to swing with the horse, rotating posteriorly and anteriorly. If the *seat is too deep* for the individual pelvis, the rider is trapped and unable to move with the horse.

Rider's Trunk

When analyzing a saddle for a rider and detailing rider issues, the pelvic orientation leads upward to the rider's trunk. When viewed from the front or back, lateral bending and twisting of a rider's trunk can be either an indicator or a cause of pelvic misalignment. There will be shortening of one side of the ribcage. This leads to a dropped shoulder on that side. Then the seat bone on the shortened side of the rider has less weight on it than the opposite side. **Illustration 4.4 Rider's Asymmetry Due to Lateral Bending** shows how the upper body can deform and contort.

Muscle groups in a rider's trunk, especially the abdominal muscles, are commonly referred to as *core muscles*. They are what allows riders to position themselves in a dynamic state as the horse moves independently. When a rider can effectively maintain balance and coordination while also supporting a horse's movement and influencing the horse in a positive way, we say she has an *independent seat* (and yes, the trunk plays a key role in this!). To have an independent seat, a rider's feel or proprioception must be developed, accurate, and immediate. The rider must be elastic enough to allow for the horse's movement without blocking it, meaning

When the seat of the saddle is too deep, it can "trap" a rider's pelvis and prevent it from moving with the horse.

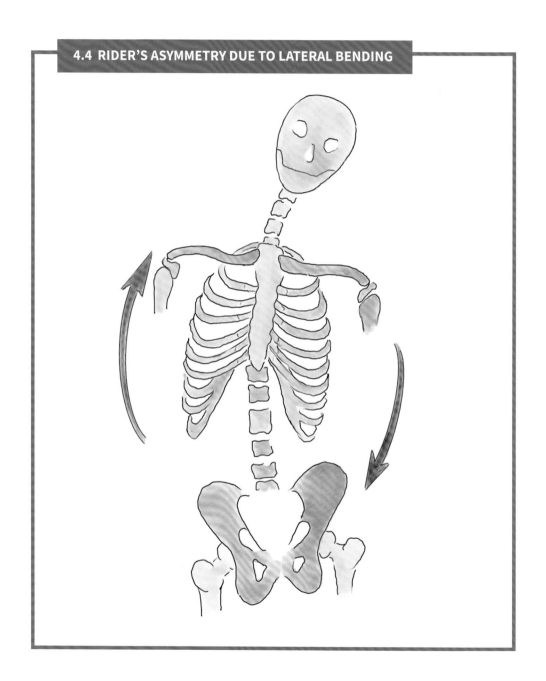

4.4 RIDER'S ASYMMETRY DUE TO LATERAL BENDING

the rider must move *with* the horse. To accomplish this, the rider needs balanced strength in key trunk muscle groups: the *obliques, transverse abdominus, rectus abdominus* in the front of the trunk, and *erector spinae* along both sides of the spine in the back of the torso. These are shown in **Illustration 4.5 Muscles in Rider's Torso**. (Adjoining muscle groups are included in this illustration, and it is useful as a rider to identify muscles that are repeatedly painful, as that is an indicator of compensation, whether it be rider compensation for poor saddle fit or horse compensation for structural difficulties, or something else altogether.)

When students under a particular trainer are encouraged to get the same style saddle as their trainer (a frequent occurrence) they are putting themselves at a disadvantage. Body types are different, so individual analysis is necessary, yes—but in addition, the use of musculature, including the core, differs by experience and ability. Dr. Russell MacKechnie-Guire, founder of Centaur Biomechanics (centaurbiomechanics.co.uk), has demonstrated that advanced riders have increased contractions or activation of the *rectus abdominus* and *erector spinae*. Novice riders, on the other hand, often have increased contractions of the *rectus abdominus* without the balancing *erector spinae*, resulting in a gripping thigh to compensate for an unstable upper body. The novice rider then often benefits from a deeper, more defined saddle seat and support for a correct leg position.

The use of musculature differs by rider experience and ability, so saddle fit requires individual analysis.

That brings us to the rider's leg and how it is accommodated by the saddle.

Rider's Leg

It is best to begin by identifying a normal pelvic alignment off the horse (see p. 32) with a normal orientation of the rider's hip, leg, and foot. In this case of straight alignment, it is the muscular development of the thigh that tends to dictate a rider's leg position. In **Illustration 4.6 Rider's Leg** you can see a "non-gripping leg," with a focus on the thigh area. The

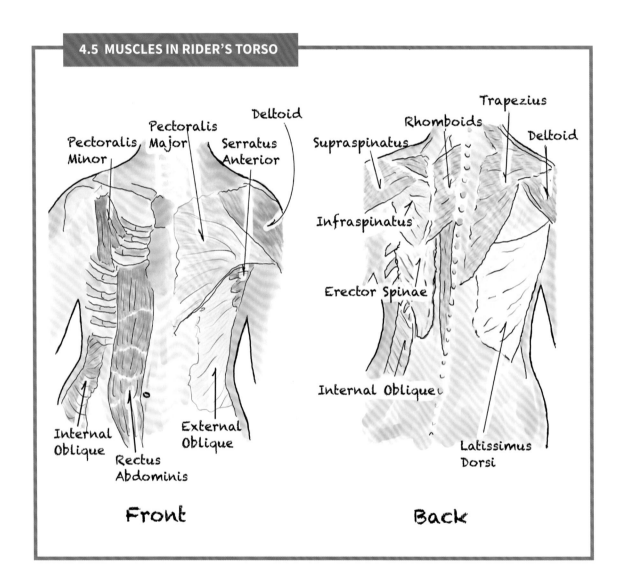

Front

Back

Advanced Rider's Non-gripping Leg (Adductor Magnus Relaxed)

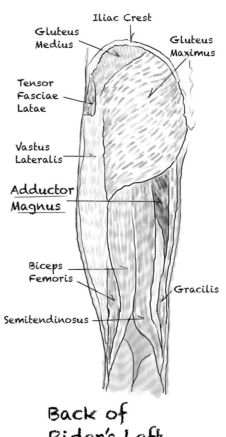

Iliac Crest

Gluteus Medius

Gluteus Maximus

Tensor Fasciae Latae

Vastus Lateralis

Adductor Magnus

Biceps Femoris

Gracilis

Semitendinosus

Back of Rider's Left Hip and Thigh

adductor magnus, the leg muscle that "grips" when on horseback, is largely inactive in more advanced riders. Novice riders, meanwhile, generally have a more developed *adductor magnus* to compensate for an unstable upper body. With a normal skeletal alignment, good instruction and supporting exercise, the novice rider will develop a good leg position—and a well-fit saddle will reinforce it.

Complications with Rider Leg Structure

Things get more complicated with skeletal deviations. In my case, a congenital disorder caused hip dysplasia, an anterior pelvic tilt, and knee misalignment, making it impossible for me to obtain correct leg position. It is interesting to note that despite these challenges, the horses I rode had no trouble interpreting my aids because they were consistent. What was problematic for me, however, was saddle design. Most saddles were painful in many ways because they worked against my peculiar skeletal conformation. This, of course, made me very aware of rider alignment and the need to design saddles to allow for the rider's unique circumstances, while maintaining proper fit for the horse.

Watching a rider walk, stand, and rest provides clues as to how that individual will sit and move when mounted. Forcing a rider into an "optimal" position, rather than accommodating her body with saddle fit, could cause pain, damage, and eventually lead to a rider to no longer desiring to ride horses.

Difficulties with Rider Symmetry

When analyzing rider posture—as mentioned, an important part of the saddle fitting process—I have noticed many variations of rider compensation and distortion. Why is the optimum riding position so difficult to obtain? It seems easier to address asymmetry in horses, both to define it and to correct it, than it is to consider asymmetry of the rider.

One good reason stems from horses evolving as prey animals with their main defense being an ability to run. Their bodies evolved for that purpose. Humans, meanwhile, are much more complex. Our upright posture allows an enormous degree of variability in movement. We can create different movement strategies based on needs and limitations. While that allows riders to be versatile and adaptable, it makes it very difficult to develop even, balanced, and symmetrical riding on a consistent basis. It is realistic to understand that many riders, particularly those at higher competition levels, likely experience pain and functional asymmetry. That pain and functional disturbance will change over time, depending on the different horses being ridden, the quality of the trainers the rider has access to, the ability of the rider to access outside therapeutics like body work and physical therapy, and (yes!) the variety of saddle options (and the fit of those saddles) available to them. Saddle design targeted to each rider is paramount to allowing a rider to function well without pain. But once a good choice in saddle has been made, the effort to ensure proper fit doesn't stop. Saddles require maintenance, horses change shape, riders change their position, and have corrective surgery and joint replacement. All these factors, among others, require a saddle to be checked and adjusted at a minimum of six-month intervals. Sometimes the changes that occur require a saddle change. It is my hope that the methodology I present in the following chapters can help make that change a successful one.

Additional Research and Innovation

Concern for the well-being, comfort, and longevity of our horses has pointed researchers in the direction of studying rider effectiveness. It is clear that unless riders are riding effectively and without pain, horses are not able to function at their best. I believe this needed understanding of the influences of the rider will ultimately influence saddle design.

5 Saddle Safety

It is crucial for any handler of a saddle—whether it be a groom, rider, trainer, or saddle fitter—to understand basic safety checkpoints. Failure to assess these checkpoints may result in broken or damaged tack, an uncomfortable or unsafe rider, a horse in pain or unwilling to perform, or all these things at once. The purpose of this safety section is to not only name these checkpoints, but to give you basic instructions for preserving your saddle and keeping it in good condition.

Tree Safety

When is it important to check the condition of the tree of the saddle?

✳ **Before purchasing a saddle, whether used or new.** Even if a saddle is new, damage can occur during shipping or handling, so let the buyer beware!

✳ **Every few months.** More frequently if your saddle is at a barn where other people could move, drop, or damage your saddle without your knowledge.

✳ **When problems arise with the fit of the saddle.** Sometimes this shows up as behavioral changes in the horse or position difficulties for the rider.

✳ **Immediately** when the saddle has been dropped or when it was on a horse that has fallen or rolled.

The *rails* of the saddle's tree run between the pommel and the cantle (see **Illustrations 2.1 and 2.2**, pp. 6 and 8). It is important to check this area in any of the above-mentioned scenarios, as the rails can break or distort, thus compromising the structural integrity of the saddle.

To check the condition of the rails (**Illustration 5.1 Checking the Tree of the Saddle Through the Rails**):

1. Place the pommel of the saddle against the middle of one thigh.

2. Hold the cantle with one hand.

3. Take your free hand and press down on each side of the tree (left and right) along the length of the tree.

4. While you're doing this, apply upward pressure on the cantle.

If...	Then...
The tree gives a little under your hand...	...the tree is fine and in good condition.
The tree gives to the point of light flexibility...	...the tree is okay but perhaps is showing signs of use and age. Check it regularly.
The tree is very flexible, is moving through the seat area in an unnatural way, or making noise like clicking or squeaking...	...the tree is likely damaged and cannot be used. It is best to have a skilled saddler appraise the saddle. Continued use with apparent damage will injure the horse. (Note that it may be possible for the tree to be repaired or replaced by a skilled saddler.)

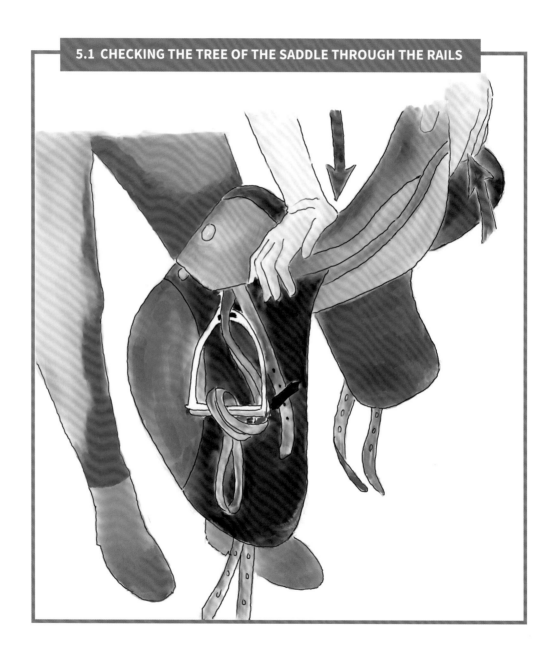

The *points* of the saddle's tree are located in the area across the front of the saddle (see **Illustration 2.2,** p. 8). To check the condition of the tree at the points (**Illustration 5.2 Checking the Tree of the Saddle Through the Points**):

1. While in a standing position, place the back of the saddle against your torso.

2. Put a hand on each side of the saddle in the front, grasping the saddle panels and flaps.

3. Pull your hands away from each other. The saddle should not move at all and should not make any noise. When the area at the points of the tree *does* move, it is generally on one side only and indicates that a point has broken or come loose. It is important *not* to use the saddle until it has been repaired by a skilled saddler.

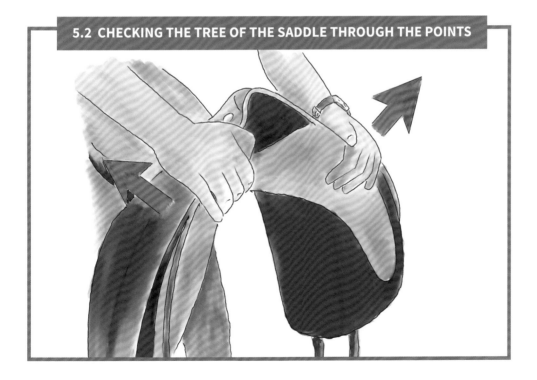

5.2 CHECKING THE TREE OF THE SADDLE THROUGH THE POINTS

Billet Safety

The *billets* of your saddle (see **Illustration 2.1**, p. 6) should be checked every time the saddle is thoroughly cleaned or at least once a month. It is normal for billets to wear and need repair, and they are easily replaced by a saddler. To check them:

1. Visually inspect the stitching of the billets at the top where they attach to the nylon webbing that is secured to the saddle tree. Check the top and the bottom of the stitching to make sure the thread is not broken or worn through.

2. Look at the leather of the billets to make sure it is not cracked or scratched beyond just the surface. Some shallow wrinkling and wear lines are normal because the leather must bend to go through the buckles of the girth, but those wrinkles should not extend into the flesh of the leather. If they do, they are *cracks*, which warrant repair.

3. Look at the holes in the billets. While there will be some wear that changes the shape of the holes, those holes should not be elongated to more than 1.5 times their original size. Elongated holes mean the leather has weakened. Any tearing along those holes means the billet should be replaced.

4. Feel the leather to make sure it is adequately clean and supple. If the leather is too dry, it will crack. If it is too oily or greasy, it will stretch. Both are safety hazards.

Stirrup Bar Safety

There are a few different kinds of *stirrup bars* (see **Illustration 2.1**, p. 6). Some are a simple curved shape, and some have a straight bar with a hinged tip that can be left "open" or moved upward to "lock" the stirrup on. Unless you have a specific reason for extra security (like riding up and down hills cross-country), the hinged bar should be "opened" flat so that the stirrup can come off if you fall off your horse and get hung up in the stirrup.

Some stirrup bars are adjustable in terms of where the stirrup leather can be placed to adjust for the leg of the particular rider. In all cases, the stirrup bar should be firmly anchored. Any ability to move or wriggle the bar with your hand indicates that it needs to be repaired by a saddler. Stirrup bars are secured to the tree of the saddle by metal rivets, which are much like large nails without the pointed end. If a rivet comes loose, it needs to be repaired immediately and the saddle should not be used until the repair is made. There are instances where a stirrup can get stuck—for example, on a gate—and the horse's motion forward pulls against it. When this happens, which is surprisingly frequent, the stirrup bar on that side generally becomes deformed or gets pulled loose. A saddler then needs to access the saddle tree and replace the stirrup bar into the tree. Simply hammering the stirrup bar back in place is seldom sufficient, and more importantly, it weakens the deformed metal further, making the stirrup bar even more unsafe for the rider.

Tree and Panel Straightness

It is important to frequently check the straightness of the tree and the panels. Wooden trees can twist, which ends the life of the tree, since a twisted tree cannot be repaired. But for those who are not professional saddlers, it is nearly impossible to determine if a tree is twisted versus whether the panels are deformed, so I have joined the two issues by the following test:

1. Stand outside in the sunlight, directly facing the sun.

2. Place the saddle pommel-down in front of your toes with the surface of the saddle seat facing your legs.

3. Look straight down and visually check to see if the saddle is lined up symmetrically. The middle of the cantle should appear to be directly over the middle of the pommel (**Illustration 5.3 Viewing Saddle Symmetry**). The panels on the left and right should have the same thickness and orientation. When you note a difference in symmetry, the saddle should go to a skilled saddler who may have to take the panels off the tree to determine if the tree is twisted. If a flocked panel is asymmetrical, it will need to be reflocked. If it is a foam panel, the foam needs to be replaced.

4. For flocked panels, feel their consistency with one hand on each panel. They should be smooth without lumps or holes noticeable beneath the leather. Both sides should feel the same. Because flocking is done by hand, some minor variability is normal, but it should be slight. Any unevenness in the panels translates to pressure points to your horse. Flocking shifts so it needs to be adjusted regularly—every three to six months. It should be stripped out and replaced every three to five years, depending on usage.

Panel Attachment

The panels of the saddle are attached to the tree by virtue of stitching or lacing at the pommel and the cantle. This can come loose or break, but it is easily repaired by a saddler. The lacing can be inspected by visually checking both the front and back of the saddle. The panels should fit so tightly that most of the time you cannot see the stitches holding them next to the tree.

Knee Roll and Thigh Block Attachment

There are many different kinds of *knee rolls* and *thigh blocks* (see **Illustration 7.5,** p. 85). Unless you are talking to a saddler or saddle manufacturer, the terms are used interchangeably. You will generally see a line of stitching around the roll or block, holding it to the flap or sweat flap of the saddle. When that stitching looks loose or frayed or if the roll or block

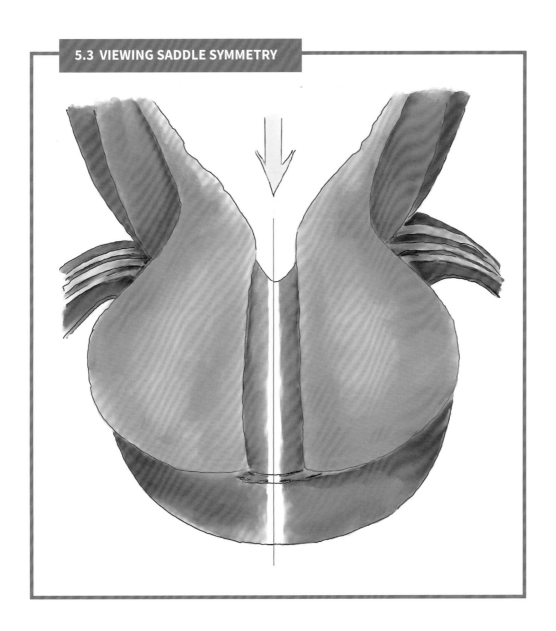

does not feel secure, it can easily be repaired by a saddler. It is best to address this before the roll or block deforms, which will happen if it is used but not repaired.

Leather Condition

The overall quality of your saddle's leather should be regularly checked, and your monthly "super-cleaning" and conditioning is a good time to do this. (See chapter 11 and **Illustration 11.1**, p. 137, for a step-by-step reference.) Leather is really tanned animal skin, and just like your skin, it needs to be cared for. The pores need to be cleaned and it needs hydration. The type of hydration and frequency of application depends on the user's environment. Dusty, dry Colorado is quite different from soggy Ireland, so those of us riding in Colorado need to clean and condition our saddles more frequently. When leather is constantly covered with dirt and dust, oils will be sucked out, resulting in a loss of elasticity and the potential to crack. Overconditioning and oiling, on the other hand, can cause dirt to stick to the leather, thus creating a substance not unlike axle grease. The leather gets blocked from the air and essentially rots beneath the dirt, getting soggy, flabby, and weak.

New leather feels smooth and strong, but stiff. Leather that has been used but well cared for similarly feels smooth and strong but no longer stiff, so it conforms to the shape of the horse and rider. It is true that leather gets better with use and age, but only if it is well cared for.

When caring for your saddle and checking the leather, be sure to turn the saddle over to check all surfaces. Quite often I see saddles that are nicely cared for on the top but cracking and dry on the bottom. The bottom of the saddle must conform to your horse's shape and can't do so if it is dry (see more about this in chapter 11, p. 136, where I discuss saddle maintenance).

Most saddlers are happy to check the condition of your saddle leather in order to help you with appropriate care.

Routine Safety Checklist

Use **Illustration 5.4 Saddle Safety Checklist** as a visual reminder of the areas to regularly check on your saddle. Keep this book in your tack room or grooming area where you can check it easily and often! (See also chapter 11, p. 136, for information on saddle maintenance and storage.)

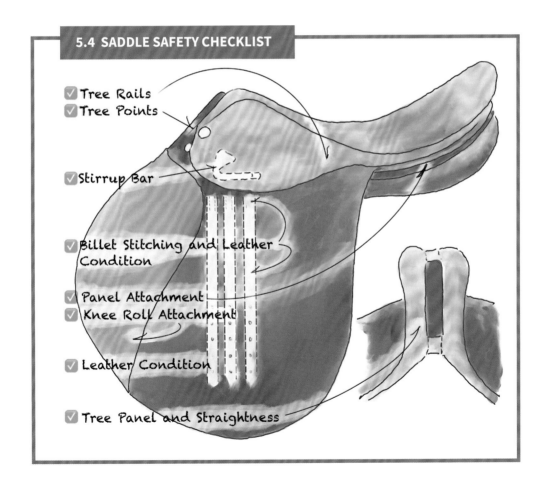

5.4 SADDLE SAFETY CHECKLIST

- ✓ Tree Rails
- ✓ Tree Points
- ✓ Stirrup Bar
- ✓ Billet Stitching and Leather Condition
- ✓ Panel Attachment
- ✓ Knee Roll Attachment
- ✓ Leather Condition
- ✓ Tree Panel and Straightness

6

Saddle Fit Checklist for the Horse

Each point I present on the following pages could be a chapter on its own! I explain and illustrate how to check the fit of your saddle, but note that I focus on *basics* and *generalities* for the sake of *simplicity* and *ease of understanding*. Also keep in mind, there are many opinions and unique saddle designs, as well as plenty of dialog, that take exception to certain points.

Frequency of Saddle Fit Check

How often you check your horse's saddle fit depends on, well, your horse! Refer to the chart on p. 53 for general guidelines.

Horse Saddle Fit Evaluation: Step by Step

The single most important success tool for fitting a saddle is having a thorough, step-by-step procedure that is always followed. It may seem overwhelming at first, but like any skill, it becomes much less so once you've done it a few times.

What I have outlined here follows a logical progression. *Do not skip steps.* Read through all the steps before beginning to check your saddle's fit so you are clear on what you need to have at hand. Having an assistant is helpful. Having patience is necessary.

The horse you need to fit is:	How often to check fit and why:
The young horse that is about to be or just being started.	This horse will change over time with development so the saddle needs to be checked every two months *at a minimum*.
The developing horse that is in a training program.	As with the young horse, every two months is a good rule of thumb to do a saddle evaluation.
The competition horse.	This horse will likely change throughout the show season and the saddle should be checked at least every three months.
The pleasure horse.	This horse's work may be light and intermittent but that does not justify the horse being uncomfortable. Checking the saddle fit every six months is usually adequate.
The aging horse.	As a horse ages, gravity and the history of the horse's previous work takes effect on the back, which often drops. Many of these horses have saddles that are bridging causing pain behind the shoulder blade, at the withers and at the back of the saddle. This must be addressed. Our senior citizens require our care and their saddles need to be checked every six months.
Any other horses out there being ridden!	The general time frame to check the average horse's saddle fit is every six months.

Step 1: Step 1 The first thing you will do is a *safety check* on each saddle you are evaluating (see chapter 5 and **Illustration 5.3**, p. 49).

Step 2: Enlist your assistant (if you have one) to help keep your horse calm and *standing squarely on level ground* with his *head up* and positioned *straight ahead of his body.* This is more important than you might realize because a cocked hip or crooked neck can give false information in terms of saddle fit.

Step 3: Carefully feel along your horse's neck and back and watch for any reactions that might indicate soreness (for example, sudden movements of the ears, head, feet, or tail). Check for puffy areas or swelling. Look for white or disturbed hairs. Feel along the *girth channel* (the area where the girth goes under the belly) for signs of soreness, swelling, or girth sores. Take note if the horse consistently rests a leg or does not stand squarely as these may be indicators of discomfort. In a notebook or on your phone, note and date your observations. Regularly tracking your observations gives you important information about your horse's well-being.

Step 4: *Create a template* of your horse's back (see p. 70 for instructions and illustrations explaining how to do this). A template will give you useful information critical to problem-solving a saddle fit issue. Comparing templates over time gives you tangible proof that your horse changes shape dramatically over the course of his life, while in training, when being rehabilitated, and in response to ailments and behaviors.

Step 5: Place the saddle on your horse's back with the girth fastened but no saddle pad (**Illustration 6.1 Saddle Placement Diagram** provides a visual reference.) Tighten the girth just enough to secure the saddle yet leave sufficient room to slip your fingers under the girth and panel. I have a few important tips for *saddle placement location,* which is critical

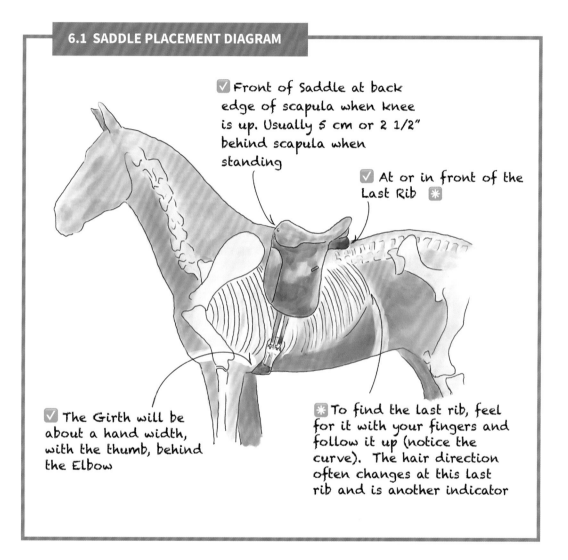

☑ Front of Saddle at back edge of scapula when knee is up. Usually 5 cm or 2 1/2" behind scapula when standing

☑ At or in front of the Last Rib ✷

☑ The Girth will be about a hand width, with the thumb, behind the Elbow

✷ To find the last rib, feel for it with your fingers and follow it up (notice the curve). The hair direction often changes at this last rib and is another indicator and often the reason a saddle isn't fitting correctly. Forget everything you may have learned about saddle placement, including terms like "sweet spot" (it sounds nice but means nothing), and follow these guidelines:

* The tree (the part you can't see but that dictates the fit of the saddle—see p. 8) must sit *behind* the horse's scapula (shoulder blade) at the point where the scapula rotates back when the horse's knee is raised. So it is good when placing your saddle to try that: with one hand, raise the horse's knee as in **Illustration 6.2 Scapula Rotation,** and feel with your other hand how the scapula glides backward, usually between 2 to 2.5 inches (5 and 7 centimeters). It is handy to mark the location of the point of the scapula (usually near the top of the withers) with a piece of chalk. Walk around to the other side of your horse, and repeat the test. Are the chalk marks in the same place on either side of the withers? If so, great—carry on! If not, use the mark that is farthest back to guide your placement of the saddle. (It is not uncommon for one side to be farther back than the other because horses have no collarbone; this means the scapulae are held by soft tissue, not bone.)

* *Determine the location of the tree points* by looking under the saddle's flap to find the *point pocket* (see **Illustration 2.1 Saddle Surface Parts**, p. 6). You will see *nail heads* (also called *buttons*) at the front (see **Illustration 2.1**). There are typically two on each side of the saddle. These nails go through the tree at the "point area" that you are trying to identify. This area needs to sit just behind the scapula when the horse's knee is *up.* That allows the shoulder to move freely when the horse is under saddle.

* When the saddle is placed correctly, the girth should be placed about a hand's width (about 4 inches or 10 centimeters) behind the elbow (to measure, place your thumb at the horse's elbow and align your fingers behind it).

When knee reaches forward, scapula rotates Back and down

✳ Placing the saddle and the girth too far forward is a common mistake. This causes significant problems that really are not solved by using a pad to raise the back of the saddle. We'll get to that in a bit (I talk about girths in detail in chapter 9, p. 108).

Step 6: The *angle of the tree points* should match the slope or angle of the widest side of the horse at the *posterior trapezius muscle* that the tree sits on. **Illustration 6.3 Viewing the Angle of the Tree Points** helps you determine this. It is helpful at this point to refer to your template (see Step 4) so that you know which side of the horse is the widest. Take a short,

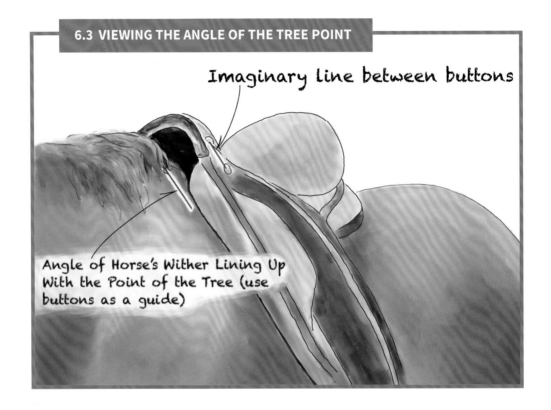

Imaginary line between buttons

Angle of Horse's Wither Lining Up With the Point of the Tree (use buttons as a guide)

straight object (a pen, pulling comb, or even chapstick) and lay it along the side of your horse's withers, touching the front of the saddle. See if the angle of the pen matches the stitch line of the point pocket or a straight object held against the two nail heads (buttons). If you are fortunate enough to have a perfect match of the withers and tree points, you can move on to the next step. If the angle of the saddle tree is more than a centimeter steeper (closer to vertical) than the angle of the horse's withers, the tree is too narrow and must be changed the for the horse. If the angle of the tree is more than a centimeter *less* steep than the angle of the withers, the tree is too wide and must be changed for the horse. Please believe me when I say, "Wider is not better." When using a saddle that is too wide by even *one* fitting size, there is loss of muscle movement toward the *front* of the saddle (specifically at the 13th thoracic vertebrae or T13). When using a saddle that is too narrow by even one fitting size, there is loss of muscle movement toward the back of the saddle (more specifically the 18th thoracic vertebrae or T18). There is a misinformed concept that fitting a saddle wider than the horse allows a horse to "grow into" the saddle or allows a horse to have unrestricted movement. In fact, recent studies quantify that the *opposite* is true because the saddle needs to be *stable* on the horse, and to have that stability, it *must* fit precisely!

Step 7: The *height of the gullet* (**Illustration 6.4 Checking Gullet Space)** without a rider is determined by running your hand through the saddle gullet next to the horse's spine. I like to find three fingers height (about 2 inches or 5 centimeters). This is the *minimum* clearance throughout the length of the saddle that allows adequate room for a horse's spine to come up into the saddle during movement. (When the rider is in the saddle, 1 inch (2.5 centimeters) height is the minimum amount of necessary room between the saddle and a horse's spine.) Under no circumstances should a saddle sit so low it comes in contact with the horse's spine, as that can cause painful damage. When you have *more* than the minimum amount of height through the gullet, as is often the case with some flat-backed breeds, such as Arabians and Quarter Horses, that is okay *as long as* the saddle passes all the other criteria listed in this fitting evaluation.

Fitting a saddle wider than the horse does NOT provide unrestricted movement— the opposite is true!

Step 8: It is important to protect the bones of the *spinous processes* and the very important nerve bundles that extend along each side of the spine, which allow for necessary proprioception. Peek back at **Illustration 3.9 Spinal Cord and Nerve Bundles** (p. 22) for a good visual of what we are trying to protect with an appropriate *width of the gullet*. The width of the gullet is measured using your hand as you did in Step 7 but positioning your fingers *horizontally* instead of vertically. Reach under the pommel and down the gullet of the saddle to feel with your fingers where it sits along the horse's spine. There needs to be

6.4 CHECKING GULLET SPACE

Throughout the length of the saddle above the spine

adequate width for the spinous processes plus an additional finger's width (about .5 inch or just over a centimeter) of room on each side of the spine. This criterion must be established from the front to the back of the saddle, along its entire length. Because saddle manufacturers now know loads more about equine anatomy and biomechanics than they did decades ago, you will no doubt run into older saddles that fail this test. For example, you will likely find a gullet that is significantly more narrow toward the back of the saddle than the front. In some circumstances, a skilled saddler can, through re-stitching, increase the width through the back of the gullet. However, there is seldom enough room in the panel design to allow for such adjustments, particularly in the case of some Warmbloods that have a lot of bone and much wider spines than the types of horses for which an older saddle may have been originally designed.

Step 9: The *saddle panels* need to be checked for even contact along the front of the saddle and along the underside of the saddle, front to back. Insert your fingertips between the horse and the saddle—you should be able to slide them in to the first joint of your fingers with little effort. Now run your fingertips along the panel in the direction of the hair growth. There should be even pressure—no tight places or gaps in the contact. Perform this test along the front and the underside of the saddle on both the left and right side of the horse as follows:

⁕ The *front panel area* is the area you were looking at when checking the angle of the tree points (see Step 6). Start your fingers at the top of the panel next to the gullet and run them downward along the panel (**Illustration 6.5 Panel Contact**). With the saddle girthed, it should seem to have nice contact all the way down the saddle.

⁕ The *underside of the panel* also needs to be checked (**Illustration 6.6 Feeling Panel and Rails of the Tree**). Note that if your saddle is not girthed as described in Step 5, your results will *not* be accurate. Reach all the way underneath the saddle flap to

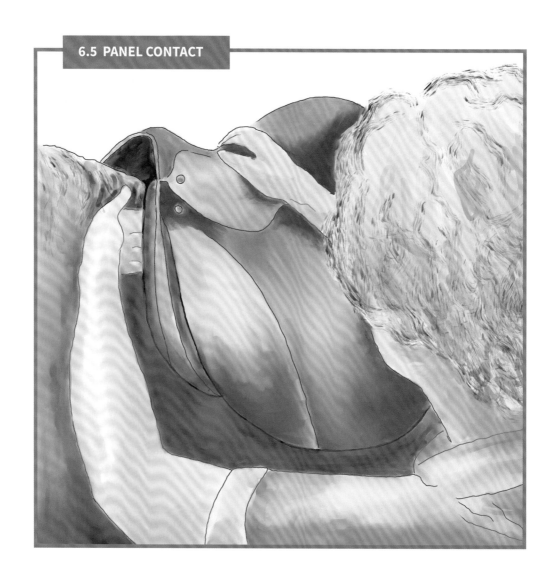

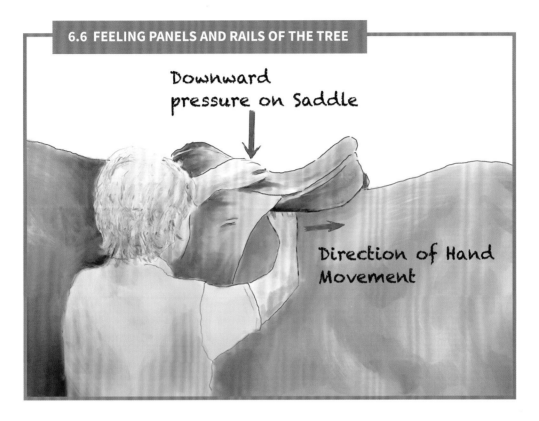

Downward
pressure on Saddle

Direction of Hand
Movement

about where the stirrup bar is located. This is important as a starting point, since this is the area that most commonly displays a fitting problem. Slide your fingertips, between the saddle panel and the horse, from the front of the saddle to the back, taking note of whether or not there is even pressure.

- When there is little or less contact in the area under the stirrup bars, that means the saddle is *bridging*. This happens when the saddle is placed too far forward and is sitting over the scapulae (see Step 2); when the tree is too tight (narrow); or when the panel flocking is deformed. Sometimes there is pressure felt under the stirrup bars but the pressure lessens as you move your fingers toward the back of the saddle. This indicates that the stirrup bars need to be pulled outward because they are too "recessed" for that horse. A skilled saddler can remedy this.

- When the contact is not extending all the way to the back of the saddle, the saddle is *floating.* This is a fitting failure because the weight of the rider is not distributed all along the panels, thereby putting excessive pressure on the horse's back toward the front of the saddle. We have to distribute the rider's weight over the entire surface of the panels in order to minimize excessive pressure. Floating also creates instability as the horse moves. The back of the saddle will likely swing left and right as well as "bounce" on the horse's back. (Compression and decompression of the saddle is normal to see at the back of the saddle with a rider, particularly at rising trot. "Bouncing" means there is space *under* the back of the panels at trot and canter.) This "shearing" movement, where the saddle does not move as a part of the horse's back, but on its own, is every bit as harmful to the horse as sustained pressure points. It is abrasive, annoying, and damaging to the horse, and it mutes the rider's aids, thus making for ambiguous communication between the two.

Step 10: The next couple of saddle fitting points involve checking the fit of the aspects of the tree that you cannot see. I have provided you " x-ray vision" by means of **Illustration 6.7 Fitting the Tree**, which shows you the tree on the horse, fitting as it *should*, and fitting in ways that it *shouldn't*. Looking at these examples will help you as you read through the following discussion and will clarify the saddle-fitting faults commonly seen. We begin with *curvature of the rails of the tree.* These must be checked using the same method I explained to check the bottom of the panels in Step 9 (see **Illustration 6.6**, p. 63). It requires inserting your fingers under the panels, and then putting pressure against the panels, which will "give way" so you can feel the *rails* of the tree (see also **Illustration 2.2**, p. 8). A palm-up hand position is helpful to feel their shape and location. As an example of why these aspects are

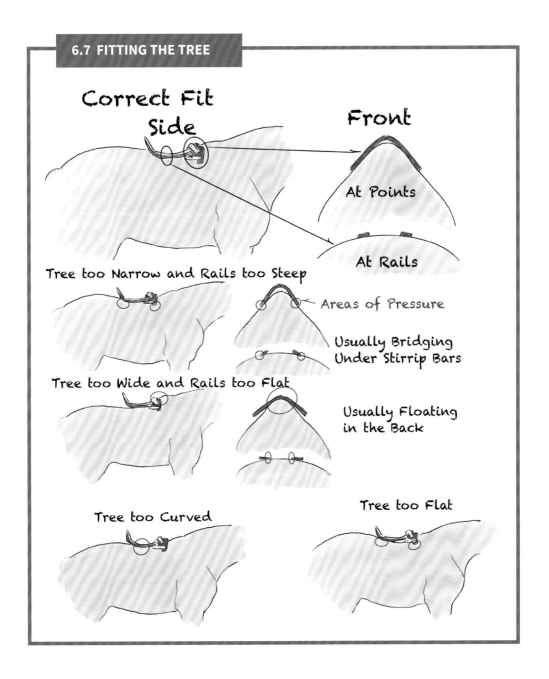

Correct Fit
Side

Front

At Points

At Rails

Tree too Narrow and Rails too Steep

Areas of Pressure

Usually Bridging
Under Stirrip Bars

Tree too Wide and Rails too Flat

Usually Floating
in the Back

Tree too Curved

Tree too Flat

important, if the tree rails are curved front to back but placed on a horse with a flat topline, like a young Thoroughbred, the saddle will float, lifting away from the horse at the back (see Step 9). Similarly, if an older horse with some "drop" in his back (an extreme case would be sway back) is ridden in a saddle with flat rails, the saddle will bridge. No amount of flocking or padding can fix a problem with incorrect fit of the tree. The flocking will quickly take on the shape of the tree and only amplify the problem. The saddle must be rejected.

Step 11: The *angle of the rails of the tree* has to be checked in a way similar to checking their curvature. Run your fingers along the saddle panel to find a spot where you can best detect the *angle of the panel,* which is dictated by the angle of the rails of the tree. Sometime a finger-pads-up position is helpful. Do you find that the angle of the rails matches the angle of the horse's rib cage? Or is it different? Check both sides (one side may be easier for you to feel than the other). When the tree has a steep angle along the rails, it might be perfect for a slab-sided Thoroughbred, but if placed on a flat-backed Quarter Horse, the horse will feel an edge, much like the edge of a butter knife, putting pressure all along the length of the tree. This often undetected situation is painful for the horse! Similarly, a flat-railed saddle designed for a broad-backed Quarter Horse will never be comfortable on a narrow Thoroughbred because the rider's weight will press along the inside edge of the panel next to the gullet. There will be no support along the outer edges of the panel, which extend outward with little or no contact with the horse's sides. The result is the horse feeling extreme pressure where the ribs attach to the thoracic spine. This problem can displace the horse's ribs.

Step 12: The *length of the saddle* should be checked on every horse and is critical to short-backed horses and ponies (**Illustration 6.8 Length of the Saddle**). I have been surprised to discover a large number of Warmbloods with extremely short backs where the length of the saddle was a problem, so don't assume that a large horse will automatically

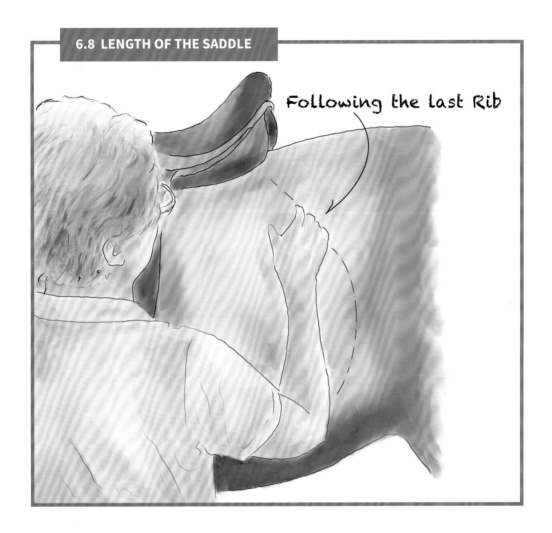

6.8 LENGTH OF THE SADDLE

Following the last Rib

pass this test. Weight can only be carried by the horse over the *thoracic spine*, which has the support of the rib cage. When the saddle extends to the *lumbar spine*, the saddle will sit on an unsupported area of the back, resulting in the potential of a sore horse and misalignment of the lumbar and sacroiliac areas (see **Illustrations 3.3 and 6.1**, pp. 17 and 55, for a reminder of the shape and location of the lumbar spinal column).

To locate the last thoracic vertebrae in the horse's spine, feel along the rib cage until you reach the final rib, and follow that rib upward. The rib does *not* go straight up but curves upward and toward the middle of the horse. You have to be careful to follow the rib accurately so you can identify if a saddle is too long for the horse's back. Many times noticing the directional change of the hair pattern in the horse's coat can help you, as this change in direction tends to follow the last rib. This is particularly helpful when you have a horse with a higher body condition score (increased fat—see p. 25) that makes it difficult to feel the rib.

Confirm your last thoracic location by the decrease in the width of the spinous process at the first lumbar vertebra. You can do this by feeling along the spine of the horse with a thumb on one side and finger on the other (a pinching position with just enough squeeze to feel the width of the spine). You will notice that the top of the spinous process within the thoracic spine area is wider than in the lumbar spine. The spot where the spine gets less wide is the point of the *thoraco-lumbar (TL) junction*—and the back of the saddle should not extend beyond this point.

Step 13: *Saddle symmetry*—left side to right side is critical. You can determine symmetry with two different tests; do both to check that your analysis is correct.

* ❋ **Visual Test:** Stand behind your horse at a safe distance with the horse standing straight and square. Stand on a mounting block if necessary in order to see over the horse's hindquarters. You will need a light source directly at the front or back of the saddle, or diffuse. You do not want it coming in at an angle. Sight down the gullet of the saddle from the back, and make sure that the center of the gullet is over the center of the horse's spine. If the gullet is to one side, double check the placement of your saddle by confirming that the middle of the pommel is over the middle of the horse's withers. If the saddle is placed correctly but is still off to one side when

viewing down the gullet from the back, consider whether the horse's *body* is symmetrical. And the only way you can know if your horse is symmetrical is to use the template you created in Step 4 (p. 72). If your horse is fairly symmetrical, the saddle is placed correctly, and the saddle is sitting to the right or left sides, we have to assume that the saddle is crooked and indicating either tree or panel asymmetry.

✳ **Analysis by Feel:** From the pommel, insert your hand to feel along the horse's spine to see if the saddle gullet follows the spine. This is a very accurate test of symmetry that requires subtlety and careful attention. It may be necessary to stand on a block for a larger horse. You will feel your horse's withers and by putting a thumb on one side of the withers and finger on the other side, you will be able to, at the same time, feel the gullet of the saddle with the top side of your hand. If you feel the panel of the saddle close to the withers on one side, but not on the other, this means the center of the gullet of the saddle is not over the center of the horse's withers. The same test needs to be performed at the back of the saddle, feeling the spinous process with a thumb on one side and finger on the other side, then noticing whether the panel comes close or touches the spinous process on one side and not the other. *The gullet should always be directly over the spinous processes.* (Note: Having your assistant keep your horse standing straight and square is critical for this test!)

What to Do with the Evaluation Results

When your saddle fails *any* of the tests explained in these 13 steps, it fails to be good enough to put on your horse. We don't work on percentages when it comes to saddle fit; when asked whether a saddle passes each of the tests, the answer must be a resounding, "Yes!" There are times I've indicated a particular issue can probably be remedied by a skilled saddler, but don't assume that will be the case.

Creating a Paper Template of the Horse's Back

The Horse Should Be...

- …groomed sufficiently for you to see and feel any hair or skin abnormalities.

- …dry.

- …calm enough to stand quietly.

- …standing square on level, flat ground.

- …in an area with good lighting.

- …holding his head straight ahead in an upward position (an assistant can be helpful for keeping the horse in position while you are taking the template).

Materials You Need

- Large graph paper or drawing paper sized about 11 by 17 inches (paper grocery bags, cut into flat sections, also work). Graph paper works best to keep the cross sections of the horse lined up straight, making the readings easier for interpretation.

- A pen or pencil that draws easily with little pressure (Sharpie® brand pens work particularly well).

- Chalk of a color that shows up well on your horse.

- A hard, flat surface to put your paper on. Tables are nice but seldom available, so I use two clipboards taped together. The clips on either end come in handy to secure the paper, especially when you are outside and it is breezy.

- A template stick that is flexible but holds its shape when you move it. What works well for me is a flexible curve ruler used by draftsmen, artists, and clothing designers. It is available in different sizes and can be found easily online, or at hardware or art supply stores. They are, however, *extremely* flexible so care is necessary to keep the horse's shape when transferring the flexible ruler's measurements to paper. (You can also use a piece of stiff fencing wire or a cut clothes hanger if you can't find the appropriate tool.) For this purpose, the stick or ruler should be about 22 inches (56 centimeters) long. Use a piece of tape or marker to mark the middle of your stick or ruler at the halfway point. From that center mark, make a mark at 4 inches (10 centimeters) and 8 inches (about 20 centimeters) of the center on both sides. You should now have five marks approximately 4 inches (10 centimeters) apart.

Basic Information to Include on the Template

- Date.

- Name of the horse.

- Any issue you want to track such as diet change, training schedule, shoeing issues, injury, or rehabilitation.

- Weight tape reading if you have a weight tape.

Template Procedure—Step by Step

Step 1: Feel each side of your horse's body, starting at the neck and working your way back to his hind end, to check for soreness or muscle spasms. Use three fingers together to apply pressure along the neck, shoulders, back, and croup in a "press–release–move–press–release–move…" pattern.

- DO NOT use a single finger or thumb; that is too much pressure at one spot. The amount of pressure you apply should be such that *you* would not be uncomfortable if it was applied to *your* body.

- DO NOT run constant pressure along the horse as you move your hand without any release; this will give you a false positive as it triggers the nerves.

Step 2: Make note of your observations on your template paper so you have them in recorded form. It takes time to develop a technique for this kind of palpation to check for soreness, but it is a very useful tool to develop and well worth the effort to learn.

Step 3: Feel along the girth channel and the horse's sternum for soreness, swelling, disturbed hair, or sores on the skin. Check both sides of the horse. (Problems in the girth area are often related to saddle fit issues.)

Step 4: From the left side of the horse, hold a piece of your chalk with your right hand, lift your horse's knee with your left hand while feeling the location of the scapula as you did on p. 57 (see **Illustration 6.2**). You will notice that the scapula rotates backward like a windshield wiper. At the point when the knee is raised to the maximum yet comfortable height, the scapula is in the rotated position. Place your right finger or the piece of chalk right behind the scapula before putting the knee down. Make a chalk mark at this point, then extend that chalk mark up to the very top of the withers so that you can see the mark from the other side of the horse.

Step 5: Repeat Step 4 on the right side of the horse, with your right hand lifting the knee and left hand holding the chalk.

Step 6: When the chalk marks from both sides line up, it doesn't matter which side you work from to complete your template. When they do *not* line up, however, work through the remaining steps from the side that has the chalk mark *farther back* toward the horse's tail. (As you will remember from chapter 3, the horse's scapula is not held in place by bone since horses do not have collarbones. It is not unusual to have one scapula positioned farther back than the other—see p. 56.)

Step 7: Lay the template stick or flexible ruler along the horse's topline (spine), with the first mark you made on the stick (closest to one end of the stick) lined up with the chalk mark behind the horse's scapula. Form the shape of the stick or ruler to follow the shape of your horse's topline by pressing the stick downward on the spine. Do so firmly enough to shape the stick but not so forcefully as to make the horse change his own shape by dropping his back away from the pressure. Make a chalk mark on the horse's back at each of the remaining four lines marked on the stick as shown in **Illustration 6.9 Drawing Template Topline.**

Step 8: Making a mental note of which end of the stick is closer to the front of the horse, carefully move the stick from the horse's topline to your template paper without changing the shape of the stick. Lay the stick on the paper along the bottom horizontal edge and trace the shape on the underneath side of the stick. Add short perpendicular lines through the tracing at each of the five marks on the stick. Number those marks "1" through "5" with "1" at the "front" (the mark behind the scapula) and "5" being the back (toward where the horse's flank would have been).

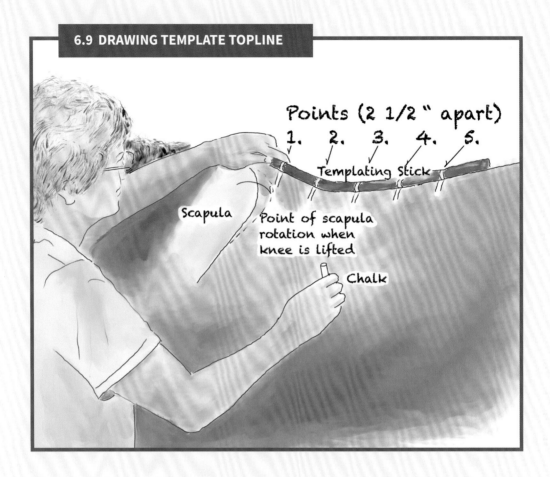

6.9 DRAWING TEMPLATE TOPLINE

Points (2 1/2 " apart)
1.   2.   3.   4.   5.

Templating Stick

Scapula

Point of scapula rotation when knee is lifted

Chalk

Step 9: Next, bend the stick at the middle mark, making an upside-down "V" shape. Hold the middle mark on the stick directly over the horse's spine aligned with the fore-most chalk mark you made on his back (**Illustration 6.10 Drawing Template Cross Sections**). Lower the upside-down "V" to straddle the horse's body, and firmly and evenly press the stick next to the horse on both sides. (You may need to stand on a stool or have an assistant help press the stick in place on the other side if your horse is tall.)

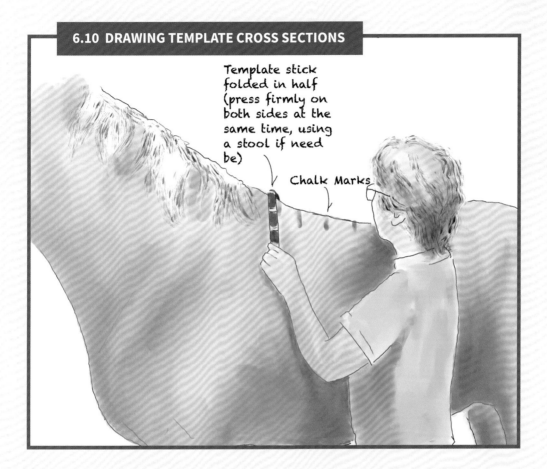

6.10 DRAWING TEMPLATE CROSS SECTIONS

Template stick folded in half (press firmly on both sides at the same time, using a stool if need be)

Chalk Marks

Step 10: Carefully lift the stick, maintaining its shape and keeping your left hand on the left side. Lay the stick on your paper toward the top of the page, but centered, with the left-hand side of the horse (your left hand) on the left side of the paper. Carefully trace the contour underneath the stick. Make a note on the paper as to which side is left and which is right. Next to the left end of that tracing write "1" (**Illustration 6.11 Template Example**).

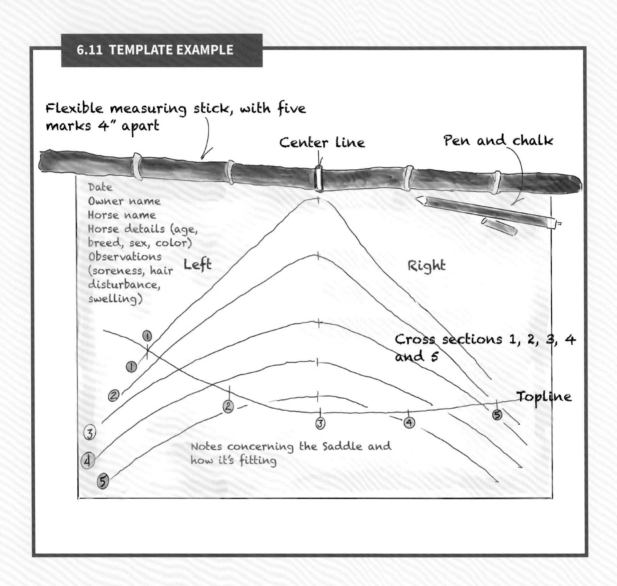

Flexible measuring stick, with five marks 4" apart

Center line

Pen and chalk

Date
Owner name
Horse name
Horse details (age, breed, sex, color)
Observations (soreness, hair disturbance, swelling)

Left

Right

Cross sections 1, 2, 3, 4 and 5

Topline

Notes concerning the Saddle and how it's fitting

Step 11: Repeat Step 10 along the other four chalk marks on the horse's back, keeping track of the left and right side, and tracing each contour under the previous on your template paper.

How to Interpret and Use Your Template

- Clearly shows you which side is more developed or wider. (using graph paper will help you keep the cross sections lined up and level making interpretation more accurate.

- Shows you areas of atrophy or lack of muscle development.

- Identifies shoulder asymmetry.

- Shows areas of soreness to monitor.

- Gives you a chronology of your horse's shape in an objective way. Templating your horse periodically, like every 4-6 months, shows you how your horse is changing, developing, compensating for or developing a problem.

- Helps you when searching for a saddle or having a saddle adjusted for your horse.

I highly recommend having a file for each horse with updated saddle-fit templates every six months, at a minimum.

7 Saddle Fit Check-list for the Rider

The basics to check the fit of the saddle for the rider can vary depending on the type of saddle (what kind of English riding you do), but most of the criteria are the same, regardless of discipline. The following guidelines apply to all saddles. (There are notations for discipline-specific fit issues.)

The guidance in this chapter assumes the saddle fits the horse well. When the saddle does *not* fit the horse well, the rider will likely be out of balance and uncomfortable, since the horse will be tight in the back with an uneven stride that lacks fluidity.

Rider Saddle Fit Evaluation—Step by Step

Step 1: *Seat size* is one of the first criteria to check. Saddle size is measured in inches from the middle of the top nail or button, diagonally across to the middle of the cantle as shown in **Illustration 7.1 Measuring Saddle Seat Size**. To determine a seat size that is comfortable for you, the general rule is you want to have a hand's width (about 4 inches or 10 centimeters) in front and in back of your bottom when sitting in the saddle. Consider, for example, Illustration **7.2 Rider Fit in a Dressage Saddle**, which demonstrates how there can be 4 inches of saddle visible in front of you and about 4 inches of space behind you (the same is true for a trail saddle). A jumping saddle seats you in a more forward position (**Illustration 7.3 Rider Fit in a Jump Saddle**) when you make that measurement, so tends to

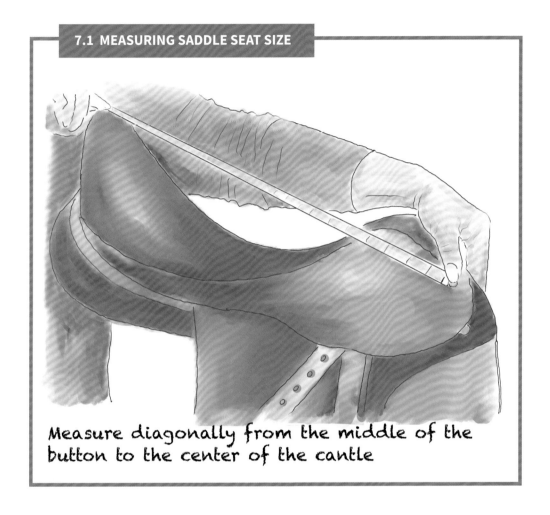

7.1 MEASURING SADDLE SEAT SIZE

Measure diagonally from the middle of the button to the center of the cantle

fit a little "tighter." There will be deviations from this guideline for saddles that are deeper or saddles with large knee rolls so comfort and practicality are the final criteria. *A word of warning:* if you are comfortable in a particular 17-inch saddle, for example, *don't* assume another manufacturer, or even another model of saddle from the *same* manufacturer, with the same size will be correct! You must try the saddle out and ride in it!

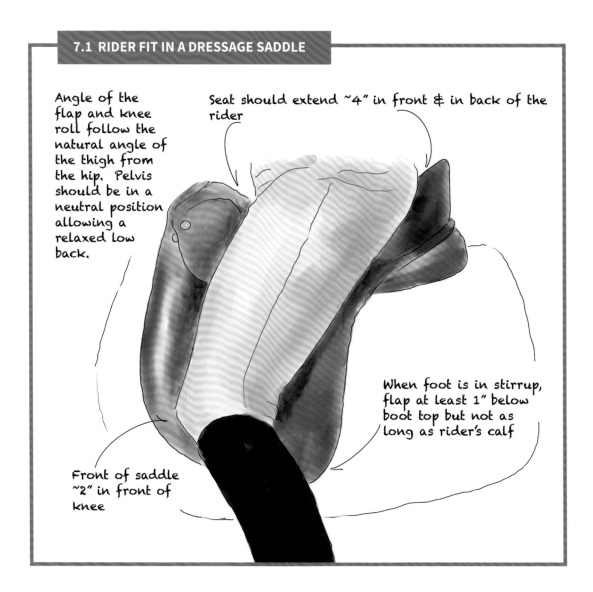

Angle of the flap and knee roll follow the natural angle of the thigh from the hip. Pelvis should be in a neutral position allowing a relaxed low back.

Seat should extend ~4" in front & in back of the rider

When foot is in stirrup, flap at least 1" below boot top but not as long as rider's calf

Front of saddle ~2" in front of knee

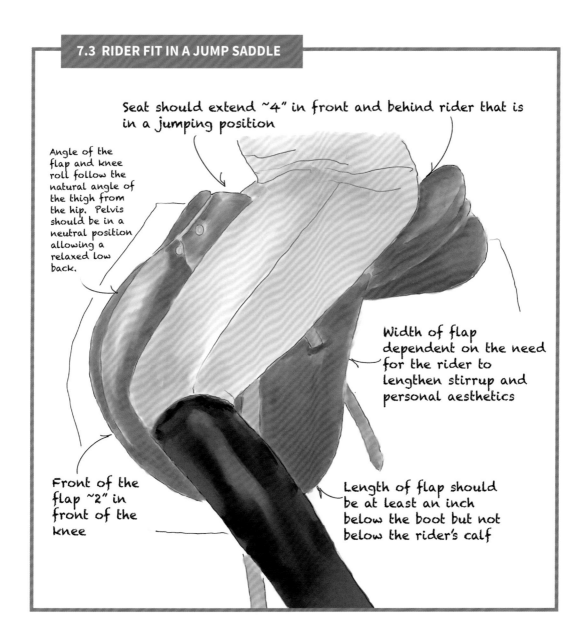

Seat should extend ~4" in front and behind rider that is in a jumping position

Angle of the flap and knee roll follow the natural angle of the thigh from the hip. Pelvis should be in a neutral position allowing a relaxed low back.

Width of flap dependent on the need for the rider to lengthen stirrup and personal aesthetics

Front of the flap ~2" in front of the knee

Length of flap should be at least an inch below the boot but not below the rider's calf

Step 2: *Length of flap* correlates to the seat size in the manufacturing process (**Illustration 7.4 Defining the Flap**). You can look at **Illustrations 7.2 and 7.3** again to see the typical flap for a "long" leg position (dressage, trail) and "short" leg position (jumping disciplines) respectively. But in addition, as the seat size increases, the length of flap gets proportionally longer. Manufacturers of high-quality saddles often offer options to both flap length and *flap angle* (which I discuss next). The length of the flap should protect the rider's upper leg and be long enough that it doesn't interfere with a rider's boot. When a rider has a boot that is too short in the calf or a flap that is too short for her leg, the top of the boot can get stuck on the flap and interfere with the rider's leg aids. Individuals may need a shorter or longer flap than the standard length. An *extra-long flap* is usually a half-inch longer, an *extra-extra-long flap* is usually another half-inch longer yet, and the reverse is the case for flaps that are shorter than standard.

> *It is important the rider is comfortable and not forced into a position by the saddle.*

Step 3: The *angle of the flap* should follow the *natural*, desired angle of the rider's thigh, as seen in **Illustrations 7.2 and 7.3**. When a rider is jumping large jumps, the flap needs to have a more forward angle to facilitate a shorter stirrup. When a rider is in a jumping saddle but mostly rides on the flat, the flap is generally straighter and the stirrup is longer. A dressage rider needs some angle to the thigh but requires a longer stirrup length, so in general, the flap is fairly straight. Again, it is important that a rider is comfortable and *not forced* into a position by the saddle. The rider needs to be able to move and change position freely in the saddle, since that is necessary to follow the movement of the horse. (Note: *Monoflap* or standard *dual flap* options are available in many saddles, letting the rider chose whether she prefers less saddle bulk under the leg. Monoflaps are designed to eliminate the sweat flap next to the horse. They feel quite different for a rider than a dual flap saddle, so it is important that the rider try such a saddle before committing. Monoflap versions are

A. Length of Flap, inches, often the same as the seat size
B. Width of Flap, inches
C. Xtra long, usually 1/2" longer
D. XX Long, an additional 1/2"
NOTE: Can also have short or XShort
E. Xtra Forward, usually an additional 1/2 " extended forward
F. XXforward, an additional 1/2 " more forward
NOTE: Can also have straighter flap

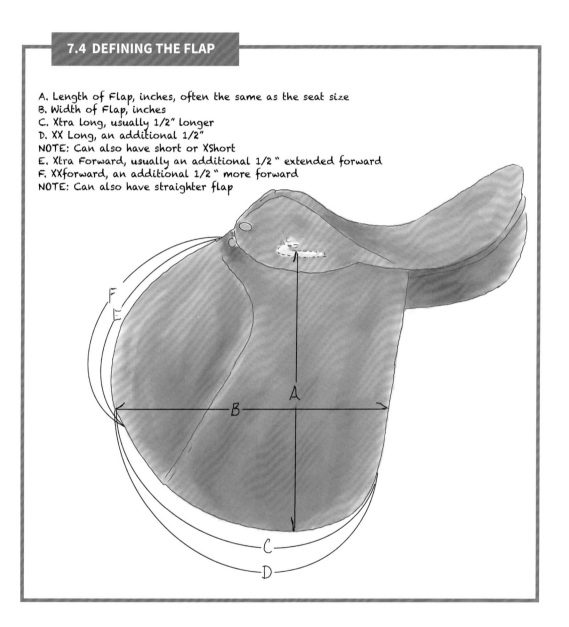

generally not favored in hunt seat circles, but they are common for cross-country and for jumpers. They have also become popular for dressage, particularly when a rider prefers a closer feel to her horse.)

Step 4:   The *location of the knee roll* and *thigh block* (when there is one) is critical to the success and comfort of the rider (**Illustration 7.5 Defining Thigh Block and Knee Roll Placement**). The size of a thigh block is less important than the location. In **Illustrations 7.6 and 7.7 Common Rider Fitting Faults**, **Short Stirrup and Long Stirrup** respectively, you can see a few common problems with knee rolls and thigh blocks. Not allowing the necessary movement of the rider's leg can limit the rider's ability. A large number of riders have asked me to put larger blocks or *external blocks,* which are blocks on the outside of the flap that directly contact the rider's leg, on their existing saddles. When discussing the reason for the request, the answer always comes back to *feelings of insecurity*. The insecurity often arises because the saddle is not balanced on the horse or does not fit the horse. Not only does this result in instability, it also can cause backs to brace against rather than absorb movement in *both horse and rider.* However, thigh blocks can cause additional issues. For example, when a block is placed in front of the leg and is too low on the thigh, it can bruise and block the rider's knee and actually *cause* instability in the lower leg.

The idea of a knee roll or thigh block is to support the desired leg position and assist the rider in stability while being unobtrusive. In all styles of saddles, the perfect knee roll or thigh block position is one that the rider doesn't notice while riding but that assists the rider when necessary. Leg support for all saddles can be in the form of a *knee roll*, a padded area in front of the knee area (commonly the only option until more recently), a *thigh block* (the blocks are of a more solid foam material covered with leather available in different shapes and sizes), or a *back block*, used in jumping saddles to keep the rider's lower leg from swinging back. The discipline will dictate which rolls or blocks are desired. Many saddle manufacturers now offer blocks that attach to the saddle surface with Velcro so the block

Placement Under Flap

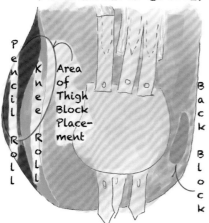

Blocks can be referred to as: knee rolls, thigh blocks, pencil rolls, etc. They are commonly under the flap as shown. (Note: dressage and polo saddles do Not generally have a back block)

External Placement

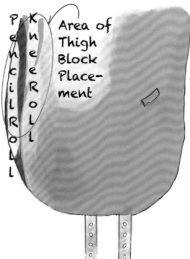

External block placement is on top of the flap, next to the rider's leg. This type of block is used for dressage saddles (as shown), jumping saddles and endurance saddles.

Size and shape of blocks are hugely variable. When they are attached with Velcro, they are adjustable.

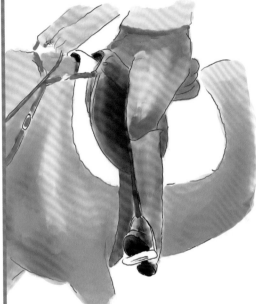

Bracing leg forces rider behind horse's center of balance. Rider's leg can't relax around the horse.

Common with young and petite riders in a saddle that is too large, flap too long or flap too forward.

Seen in many general purpose saddles where the stirrup bar is placed more forward.

A saddle that is sized incorrrectly and too small in the seat forces rider into a compressed position, often with too much weight on the pubic bone.

The flap here is too small forcing the rider's leg over the knee roll. This causes the back of the leg to pull upwards.

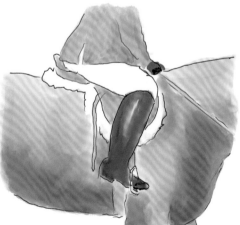

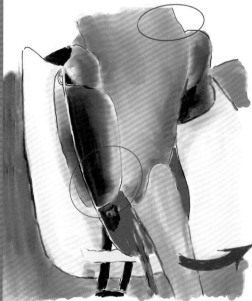

The knee block is interfering with the rider's leg:
- Puts pressure on the knee
- Lower leg gets pushed outwards
- Foot swings back with every stride
- Rider hollows low back to get shoulders back
- Rider risks pain and damage to knee and low back
- Horse can't understand rider's unclear aids, is blocked from forward movement, tends to hollow the back

The saddle is too small and the flap is too straight for the rider:
- The rider is very skilled and has to place her knee over the knee roll to place her leg at the girth
- By putting the knee over the knee roll the lower leg rotates with toe out and heel on the horse
- This causes the hip to be torqued and stiff
- The rider will likely have hip pain and will be working harder than necessary
- The horse will become dead to the spur which is always on

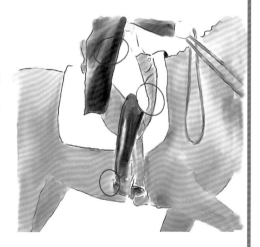

location can be fine-tuned, moved, or removed. This is ideal for a progressing rider or for multiple riders using the same saddle.

Step 5: *Depth of seat* is a growing issue for sport horse riders who are faced with riding horses with big, expressive gaits. A deeper seat is thought to give the rider more security and better definition of the center of balance. The individual rider's preference determines whether this is desirable. In jumping, it is important that the seat allow the rider to rise into a two-point position so a deeper seat can be a hinderance. The location of the deepest part of the seat is critical to rider balance so when the saddle is too large or too small, the consequences are grim. Because seat size is a defined measurement from the nail head to the middle of the cantle, seat depth (which is not a measured feature but refers to the pommel and cantle rising up above the sitting surface of the saddle) has to be considered when choosing an appropriate seat size for the rider. The deeper seat generally requires a larger seat size. (Keep in mind not every manufacturer measures the seat size accurately.)

Step 6: *Type of leather or synthetic material (sometimes called vegan leather)* is a surprisingly important variable in choosing a saddle. There are many options, such as *smooth cowhide*, which wears well and looks great over time but can be a little slick, or *double-stratum calfskin*, which is cowhide underneath with calfskin laminated and stitched over the top. The calfskin gives a naturally grippy feel and a broken-in quality to the saddle and is generally only used on the flap. Most of the time calfskin is not desired on the saddle seat since it often wears prematurely. Calfskin must be taken care of and will not last as long as cowhide. *Buffalo leather* offers a happy medium since it is grippy with a broken-in feel but long-lasting when the quality is good. Buffalo does not shine, however, giving the leather a dull look. It also is quite porous and collects dirt more easily. Synthetic materials used for saddles have evolved to include materials looking much like leather in texture and color. The advantage is cost and reduced need for care, along with durability. A *suede synthetic,* now a popular option, provides grip to the rider along with other attributes, but it will never have the classic look of a leather saddle.

Additional Tips for Fitting the Small or Young Rider

Saddle fit is a particularly important issue with petite adults and children as shown in **Illustration 7.8 Fitting Children and Petite Adults in Saddles** where the tendency is to have them ride in saddles that are too big. The outcome of wrong sizing is the inability to use or develop the correct riding position. In children, this is carried on into adulthood as the rider often defers back to a "chair seat position" (with the leg too far forward in front of the rider's seat), which is usually the result when a saddle is too large. Unlearning this behavior is very difficult. More importantly, it is a practice that is unsafe because the rider is not balanced. Plus, the horse, of course, objects to the reins being used for balance instead of a subtle means of communication.

   I have found working with young riders to select or modify their saddles has been particularly rewarding. It has also been a challenge of balancing objectives:

✳ Young riders often have tricky horses to fit since many are ponies that are wide with short backs, or older horses with dropped (swayed) backs. The rule is to *always fit the horse first* before putting a young rider into a saddle, for all the reasons we have already discussed. Particularly with a young or inexperienced rider, you do not want the horse to be uncomfortable and unable to be cooperative.

✳ After fitting the horse, you need to address each of the criteria that were identified earlier in this chapter, plus consider:

   • Seat size has to be correct, or the rider will be unable to find the center of balance.

   • Flap length shouldn't be too long, as that will make it so much harder for the horse to feel the rider's leg aids and will make it even harder for the rider to get her legs around the horse.

Many times the saddle is too big. When this happens:

The flap is under the entire leg so the horse can't feel the rider's leg well.

The deepest part of the seat is too far back so the rider is in a 'chair seat' with the feet braced forward.

With the seat too far back, the rider gets left behind the horse's motion, using the reins for balance.

Use the same guidelines when fitting petite adults and children even though children will grow out of the saddle. The outgrown saddle can be easily sold if it has been taken care of.

By providing a correctly sized saddle it is possible to learn a correct and secure position. It will be safer and more comfortable.

Children should have safety stirrups, safe equipment and good helmets that fit correctly.

- There is a little latitude with knee roll placement, since it can be a little farther away from the leg, as long as the seat is balanced and the flap length and angle are correct. The ideal saddle would have Velcro knee rolls or thigh blocks that can be moved as the child grows.

* "Grab straps" (or "bucking straps") attached at the pommel are helpful for security and to teach the young rider not to use the reins for balance.

* Safety stirrups can be added.

Indicators of Saddle Fit

We are now looking at the horse, saddle, and rider, with the rider in the saddle and engaging in their usual riding activity. Here, we will put together all the bits of information I've shared in the preceding chapters. (Discussion of girths and saddle pads follow in chapters 9 and 10—see pp. 108 and 125.) The following procedure is the process you can use when you are:

✳ Evaluating a saddle or saddles for a purchase.

✳ Considering a saddle or saddles that you already have for a new horse.

✳ Making sure the saddle you are using on your horse is adequate.

Just like when using a new cooking recipe for the first time, please read through this procedure first so you can be prepared. It will make the process easier on you and your horse. Having an assistant on the ground is very helpful!

Preparation for the Ridden Saddle Fit Test

After your saddle safety check (see p. 44) and your saddle-fit evaluation for the horse (see p. 52), saddle the horse and lead him at a walk until he is relaxed. Check the girth, adjusting as necessary, and then mount from a tall mounting block, since mounting from the ground causes unnecessary pressure on the horse's withers and spine. (It also damages the flocking of the saddle.)

From your view on your horse's back, make sure your saddle is straight, lined up over the horse's spine and that your stirrups are even. A trainer or a friend who is knowledgeable can give you feedback or take a video from the ground (in the recommendations that follow, I refer to this as your "groundperson"). I find it helpful to add strips of tape (I found white tape to be easiest to see) to the rider, down the spine, across the shoulders, and at other points that are to align when viewed from the back and from the side (**Illustration 8.1 Fit Checklist for the Ridden Horse).** Place a small piece of tape in the middle of the cantle to make the center of the saddle easier to see, and add a piece of tape on the horse's spine, just above his tail so that you can more easily see his centerline. By marking centerlines on the horse, rider, and saddle ahead of time, the following analysis will be quicker and more accurate.

General Evaluation Procedure for the Ridden Horse

✳ Be very clear about what you are going to do before putting the halter on the horse. "Reading" the horse and getting his feedback, is critical, and to do that the horse must:

- Be comfortable in his environment.

- Not be distracted.

- Have good footing in a safe arena or pasture and be allowed to be the best he can be.

✳ Evaluate *only* the saddle. This is *not* the time to consider a new bit, bridle, or other tack.

✳ Keep your session to a reasonable time. I like 45 minutes, with another 15 minutes for warming up and cooling down. If you are trying multiple saddles, have experienced people to help you evaluate the top three contenders one right after another. This way, you limit environmental variables.

* After successfully completing Fit checklist for the horse and Fit checklist for the rider:
* Evaluate at walk, trot and canter BOTH directions AND from the back asking the following questions:
~ Does the HORSE move correctly with even strides, willing to go forward, willing to listen to the rider, relaxed over the topline, tail relaxed, no facial tension or pain, take both leads at canter. If jumping, not rushing jumps or refusing.

Tape Centerline Locations at ⊛ And Shoulder to Shoulder

* At the same time, is the RIDER able to be balanced at all gaits (ear/shoulder/hip/heel), are the legs quiet yet effective, able to communicate with the horse, balance without pulling the reins, sitting STRAIGHT in the saddle with legs even, no pain (stretch is ok)

* Also at the same time, is the SADDLE (including saddle pad and girth) staying in contact with the horse and not moving up and down (bouncing) or to the side (saddle slip) or forward? CHECK FROM BEHIND at all gaits. Use tape to mark centerlines if necessary.

❋ Make sure horse and rider are relaxed and comfortable and warm up at the walk.

❋ Have the groundperson (your experienced assistant) watch the horse:

- At walk, trot, and canter on a straight line, such as down the long side of the arena.

- From the outside of a 20-meter circle, watching the horse at all three gaits in both directions.

- Over customary jumps for your horse (if jumping is an interest of yours), watching takeoff, form over the jump, and landing from both sides.

- Going up and down some hills, when trail riding is likely.

❋ It helps to make notes as you go along, answering the following questions:

- Does the horse move correctly and evenly at walk, trot, and canter in both directions?

- Is the horse relaxed, especially over his back, and listening to the rider?

- Are there any expressions of tension, like tail swishing, tight lips, or a worried eye? Are the ears forward or back?

- Is the rider balanced and able to communicate with the horse?

- Are the rider's legs quiet and even?

- Is the rider in any pain or discomfort?

- Is the rider straight in the saddle?

- Does the rider feel secure in the saddle?

- Are the saddle, saddle pad, and girth staying in place?

- Is the saddle quiet, not bouncing or moving side to side?

- Is the saddle centered throughout the ride?

- Is the saddle in the same place at the end of the ride as it was at the beginning?

✳ All these questions can be answered at the *end* of the ride because they need to be evaluated at the same time. *If, however, you or your groundperson notices right away that the answer to one of these questions is an obvious "No!" please stop.* Address the problem. If the issue is not quickly and easily solved, don't waste time and your horse's good nature with the saddle. Try another one that passes your initial tests for fitting the horse without a rider. That is why you are doing this—to weed out saddles that are *not* adequate.

Checking Movement of the Horse

Why is this mounted evaluation so critical? When the saddle is not weighted—that is, when it is observed without a rider—problems may not be evident, as long as the saddle is sitting in the correct place (see **Illustration 6.1,** p. 55). With a rider on the horse, the shape of the saddle surface next to the horse should reflect the shape of the horse, and it should sit quietly without excess independent movement on the horse's back at all gaits. Even with the added weight of the rider, the horse's own movement should be as good as his movement without the saddle or the rider. This assumes the rider is skilled, balanced, and sitting quietly. That is, obviously, a lot to assume, so we have to take the analysis piece by piece.

The shape of the saddle surface next to the horse should reflect the shape of the horse.

After going through the **Fit Checklist for the Horse, Unmounted** (**Illustration 6.1,** p. 55) and the **Fit Checklist for the Ridden Horse** (**Illustration 8.1,** p. 93), it is *critical* to examine the saddle with the rider at all gaits, both directions, with jumps or obstacles as may be required by your discipline. You may wonder why, when you have gone through the steps to check the fit in the preceding chapters, you *cannot* presume the saddle is a correct fit. Let me explain:

✳ You have checked the fit of the saddle when the horse is standing still. Since the shape of the horse changes uniquely at walk, trot, and canter, as well as over obstacles, you need to check the horse being ridden in those scenarios. Obviously, you can't run alongside the horse to check all the factors involved as the horse is moving. However, you can:

- Analyze the movement of the horse at all gaits and compare it to his free movement (without tack or a rider). Under a skilled rider, a horse's movement is often straighter, more rhythmic, more supple, and more expressive.

- Analyze the facial expression of the horse at all gaits. The horse should look focused, unbothered, confident, and comfortable.

- Pay attention to how the horse is carrying his tail. Is it relaxed, centered, and gently swinging with the movement? If the tail is stiff, held crookedly, or swishing, it may indicate a problem.

- Note whether the horse is happy to go forward in a positive way. Balking or bolting is often an indication of a tack problem, rider problem, or poor training. Always check the tack first, especially the saddle.

- Watch the horse bend in both directions. Inability to bend in one direction or another is often a saddle fit problem, as is the reluctance to take a particular lead or to change leads.

- Consider any aggressive behavior, such as bucking or rearing, as possibly a saddle fit problem, particularly when it is new behavior associated with a saddle change.

Checking the Rider

☀ The rider's position should be evaluated based on the individual rider's skill, age, and conformation, with consideration given for the rider's limitations. The saddle should help support the rider, *not* force the rider into an uncomfortable position even when it is a highly sought after position. For a rider to seek a saddle that "makes me ride like so-and-so" is unreasonable. We are all built differently, and those differences have to be accounted for.

☀ Saddles are not lounge chairs; they are not made for a passive position. When you look at the rider from the side (see **Illustration 8.1**, p. 93) you should see the rider using her core strength and balance in trot, aligned over her feet, and maintaining contact with the horse through the reins (not using the reins for balance). Saddles are made for an *active sport* where we engage our muscles, brains, and core strength to assist our horses as they are asked to engage in the discipline of our choosing. (The discipline a horse would choose would likely involve grass and pastures.)

☀ The rider should be comfortable; by this I mean there should be a lack of pain. Certainly, there will be sore muscles as we work to achieve the strength, suppleness, and fitness riding requires of us, but that is different from pain. Hip pain, back pain, inability to move freely and follow the horse's movement, neck pain, knee, and ankle pain—these are all issues that many riders deal with, yet often continue to ride through. Such painful issues may not be solved with a different saddle, but *many times, the pain is precipitated by a specific saddle.*

When a rider is in a seemingly correct position and is comfortable, but is *not effective*, it may be that the rider is "blocked" from movement by the saddle. The rider has to have the ability to move, to change positions, to give different leg aids, and to rotate the upper body while keeping the pelvis and legs in place. The fit of a saddle must accommodate the needs of the individual rider. A rider with even slight hip dysplasia, spinal misalignment, rotated knee placement, or more commonly, arthritic changes will "lock up" in certain saddles and be unable to follow the horse's movement. Not only is the rider limited in such cases, but the horse's movement is compromised, and the horse is also uncomfortable.

✳ Many riders have issues of asymmetry and those must also be addressed:

- If the rider has a true *leg length difference*, it must be detected from the ground. The side with the shorter leg needs to have a shorter stirrup. True leg length difference is *different* from a *collapsed hip* or *postural asymmetry,* and those issues should be carefully analyzed for a correction. A skilled physical therapist that understands the demands of horseback riding will be a huge benefit.

- Riders with hip angle differences need to have saddles with a narrow enough twist to accommodate the "tighter" hip or they will perpetually sit crookedly in the saddle. Care needs to be taken with the location of any knee rolls or thigh blocks so the rider does not become twisted. Both blocks need to be moved symmetrically or the rider will have no chance of becoming even. (This is where Velcro knee rolls and thigh blocks are helpful since they can be moved as the rider develops.)

- Riders with a compromised knee will often sit more firmly to the opposing side to get weight off that knee. Most of the time, this compensation is subconscious. Changing stirrup length or changing the type of stirrup should be tried to help keep the rider in the middle of the horse. Trial and error is helpful here, particularly when performed consecutively within the same ride.

✳ Riders will ride differently when they hop on after working at a desk in the office all day versus after a long walk or other activity. Take this into consideration during the evaluation.

Considering the Horse's Breed, Conformation, and Individual Gaits

When choosing a saddle, think about the horse's traits when moving. Remember though: Frustrating though it is, horses move differently from day to day. Just as we feel different from day to day, so do horses. They may be full of beans one day and sluggish the next. When they have been on a horse trailer prior to an evaluation, they may move differently, and you may find they don't move as evenly. And, as with riders who mount up after a day in the office, horses will move differently when they have been standing in a stall than they will if they have been turned out. With all this in mind, evaluate the following points related to saddle fit:

- Does the horse naturally move in a way that is smooth, flat, and linear or with more bounce, spring, and suspension? Horses that move with a great deal of suspension generally have more mobility through the spine; a saddle needs to allow for that mobility. The rider has the challenge of following and absorbing that mobility, which needs to be considered when selecting a saddle.

- Is the horse a *gaited breed*, like an Icelandic Horse, a Tennessee Walker, Saddlebred, Fox Trotter, Peruvian Paso, or Paso Fino? Some grade horses also have gaited characteristics. Gaited horses often have a longer swing to the scapula and may have more lateral movement. These characteristics may make it difficult for a saddle to stay centered over the horse's back.

    - Note: There are saddles marketed for gaited horses, as well as Arabians and Friesians, because of their unique gaits and shape. *Buyer beware*: A so-specified saddle will *not* fit all horses in that breed category! When evaluating one of these saddles, make sure it passes *all* the required criteria we have already discussed.

- Many horses have *conformational asymmetry* that is not always correctable. That doesn't mean that the horse is unable to be a functional riding horse, but such asymmetry *must* be considered when fitting a saddle, particularly in the following circumstances:

- When the horse is *sided* (has one side more developed and wider than the other), the saddle must be fit to the *widest* side. The narrower side can be *shimmed* with a shim pad (see chapter 10, p. 134) or adjusted by a saddler to match the wider side. This is important to keep the saddle centered on the horse, both when standing still without a rider and when ridden.

- When the horse has a *rotated rib cage* (the ribs are lower on one side than the other), the saddle must be fit to the side with the *higher rib cage*. Again, a shim can be used along the low side. Trial and error during the ridden phase of checking the saddle will determine how much thickness to use to keep the saddle and rider centered over the horse's spine at all gaits.

- As discussed in earlier chapters, when the horse has *uneven shoulder blade placement,* the saddle must be fit from the side with the shoulder blade that is *farther back*. Otherwise, the saddle will become crooked in the ridden evaluation and sit diagonally on the horse's back. For example, when the right shoulder blade is farther back but not accounted for during saddle fit, the *front* of the saddle will go to the *left* of center and the *back* of the saddle will go to the *right* of center; the rider's left leg will likely be farther back than the right and the rider's upper body will tend to twist.

- When the horse has a *dropped hip* on one side, the saddle needs a shim on the back half of the saddle on the *low side*. Use trial and error in the ridden saddle fitting test to determine the amount of shim to be used. Note: When shimming a saddle, trial and error is *required* with the help of a good saddle fitter or an experienced eye on the ground to help keep the saddle and rider straight. Sometimes the "cookbook solution" doesn't work because of the many variables. Don't give up. Keep trying different things that might make the horse more comfortable.

Effects of Change

Let's assume you have determined you have the perfect saddle that fits you and your horse great! After we celebrate such happy news, I need to remind you of the *equine variables* that can affect the fit of your saddle going forward:

✻ **Weight** of your horse is a big one. When a horse gains and loses weight, it is going to include the area of the topline where your saddle sits.

✻ **Condition** of the horse plays a role. As a horse becomes more fit and builds more muscle, his shape will change.

✻ **Training variations**, such as progressing up through jumping or dressage levels, advancing in any discipline, changing disciplines, or changing training regimens within a discipline will change a horse's shape.

✻ **Shoeing** changes, particularly with modifications or corrections to hoof angle, may be reflected up the limbs to the back and could change a horse's shape under the saddle. This is really important to know! The impacts from trimming and shoeing are often immediate, so check your saddle using the process outlined in this book after farrier changes.

✻ **Injuries, lameness, or any other structural issue** has the potential to dramatically change the posture and shape of your horse.

Similarly, there are *human variables* that will require saddle re-evaluation:

✻ **Weight** changes—up or down—will affect how a saddle fits the rider.

* **Condition** of a rider will change how she is able to support herself and may affect saddle balance.

* **Instructional change** is one of the biggest reasons riders change saddles. There is such a huge difference in how trainers teach and what each trainer is looking for in a rider. As that focus changes, a previous saddle may not be adequate.

* **Injury and medical issues** become a concern for a majority of riders who pursue riding throughout their lives. As the recipient of both hip and knee replacements, I can attest that once those changes are made, your existing saddle may not have the angles that you require through the twist, in the balance of the seat, and in the shape of the flap and knee rolls. Keep an open mind. When a change is needed, the cost of a saddle is insignificant compared to your medical well-being. And, when you are not riding well, your horse cannot perform at his best.

Change sneaks up on you! The majority of changes in horse and rider happen *without* the rider realizing or recognizing that the saddle may not be fitting as it should. Just because the saddle fit the horse and rider *at one time* does *not* mean that the fit is correct at the *current time*. That is why regular six-month minimum saddle checks are essential. If you had a saddle fit by a professional at the time of purchase and the saddle does not fit correctly a year later, think about what, if any, of the situations mentioned here may have developed to affect that change in fit. Also recognize that flocked saddles shift, foam panels break down, and structural changes within a saddle further compound the issues. Regular evaluations, either by a fitter or by yourself, using the guidelines in these pages, will help keep you and your horse comfortable.

CHANGE, SADDLE FIT, AND THE YOUNG HORSE

The adolescent horse that is beginning work under saddle (and changing constantly in all kinds of ways!) requires specific attention. When a developing young horse learns that saddles, girths, and other tack are uncomfortable, then the training process can be unpleasant. In an effort to avoid preventable difficulty with your young horse, please consider the following points:

When putting a saddle on for the initial experience (without a rider), you can be a bit more lenient regarding saddle fit. You may want to use an older, less expensive saddle in case the youngster rolls in it or scrapes it against a fence. Even though some aspects of fit don't need to apply in these first saddle experiences, do take care that there is room over the horse's spine and pull the saddle pad up into the pommel. Constriction over the spine will be alarming for the young horse. Take the stirrups off the saddle so they do not get hung up on a post or gate. Make sure the girth fits and is comfortable (see chapter 9, p. 108). Tighten it slowly and *do not* overtighten it—just tight enough that the saddle stays safely in place.

When a young horse learns that tack is uncomfortable, the training process can be unpleasant.

When you create a template of your young horse (see p. 70), which I highly recommend that you do, be patient and help him accept the template process, because you are going to be doing it frequently as your youngster grows and develops!

Young horses tend to have a very flat back, low withers, high croup, little topline muscle, and an ambiguous girth channel. This means a saddle will have a tendency to slide forward or roll from side to side. Follow the fit checklist for the horse (unmounted) carefully to keep the saddle more stable (see p. 52).

Check your saddle fit *every two months minimum* when you are starting your young horse. Change happens very quickly. The horse may be very underdeveloped on one side and in two months be underdeveloped on the *other* side. Shim pads will help you during this time.

As the horse's withers grow and become more pronounced, your horse's template may show less width, as though the horse has become more narrow. This is normal. When you consider the horse's skeleton, think of what is happening. The orientation of the spinous process becomes more upright as he grows. The horse becomes taller at the withers. Make sure your saddle accommodates this change.

Horses mature at different ages, even within the same breed. Once the horse has stabilized his shape, he will still change as muscles and balanced movement are developed. Change does slow, and eventually you may be able to extend your saddle evaluation and templating process to *once every three months*. Think of all your templates in those early years as "baby pictures." It is fascinating how our horses change shape over time!

Quick Reference: When Fit Is Right

The correct fit of the saddle for horse and rider is not so easy to recognize because of the many influences that come into play from both the horse and the rider's perspectives. Some horses are very stoic with a strong desire to do their job and please their rider. These are the most difficult horses to evaluate because their outstanding disposition hides many of the telltale signs of saddle fit trouble. That is why it is important to do regular evaluations as prescribed in this book, *even if it seems like nothing is wrong.* Hopefully, nothing will need to be changed, but the objective is to protect our horses.

So, when the saddle is fitting correctly, remember:

* The horse moves well and is happy in his work.

* The rider rides well and is pain-free.

* The saddle stays in the middle of the horse and does not move or change position, as does the saddle pad and the rider.

* The saddle pad (assuming the correct shape and of good quality) stays in place under the saddle.

* The girth naturally stays in the horse's girth channel.

* The sweat marks from the saddle after riding are even with no sweat over the spinal area. (There may be some areas of less sweat in the middle of the saddle above the rider's legs if it is a leisurely ride versus a training ride).

* The dirt marks on a clean saddle pad are fairly even from side to side.

✳ The horse's back is pain-free upon palpation. However, there are some trigger points such as the hock and stifle points where the horse can exhibit "referred pain" that originates under the saddle area.

Quick Reference: When Fit Is Wrong

Evaluating potential difficulties becomes complicated by the many, many factors that come into play with the health and soundness of the horse. Solving problems for a rider is somewhat easier because a rider can articulate where a problem may be coming from. With horses we need that *objective* and *subjective information* from our Horse Saddle Fit Checklist (see **Illustration 6.1**, p. 55) to separate those issues from other issues, such as subtle lameness. Objective information is important because it is factual and is not influenced by opinions or feelings. Subjective information, involving our perceptions, is necessary, as well, and best when we use it consistently.

Indicators that the saddle needs to be evaluated immediately would include:

✳ A negative attitude from the horse when a saddle is put on his back.

✳ A negative attitude when the rider mounts.

✳ Objection to the work, particularly at the beginning of the ride. Note: Pain caused by the saddle can become "numbed" during the ride, or the horse can "shut down" and block out the pain, so when a horse seems "cold-backed" (sensitive to the saddle when tacked up and early in the ride) but "works out of it," *look more closely at the saddle fit.*

✳ When the horse is repeatedly sore in the back or requires regular chiropractor attention. Note: A chiropractor or bodyworker can make strides toward solving a problem only to have the saddle un-do their work, if the fit is not corrected.

✳ Grinding of the teeth, as this is another sign of discomfort during work.

✳ Refusing jumps or bolting after jumps.

✳ Refusing a certain lead or a late lead change going in a particular direction.

✳ Refusing a gait, often the canter.

✳ Visual atrophy (muscle loss) in the back where the saddle is usually placed.

✳ Visual movement of the saddle while riding—either bouncing or moving on the back from side to side. (A video is most helpful to determine this.)

✳ Disruption of the hair pattern after riding (indicates saddle movement).

✳ Saddle pad shifting away from the saddle, usually sliding out the back.

✳ Consistently uneven sweat patterns on the horse, accompanied by uneven dirt patterns on a clean saddle pad.

✳ Areas of swelling, lumps, or sores under the saddle.

✳ Areas of swelling, lumps, or sores under the girth.

When experiencing any of the indicators that your saddle fit is wrong, keep in mind that there may be other more complicated issues at play, like lameness or shoeing issues. The saddle is one of the easiest things to check, so it should be the first thing you turn to.

9 Girths

The correct girth choice is a critical component to saddle fitting because, surprisingly enough, the saddle could be perfect for the horse, but the wrong girth will cause problems, including:

* Saddle slippage.

* Rubbing at the elbows of the horse.

* Bruising of the horse's sternum.

* Skin irritation resulting in sores.

When you have the correct girth and later change saddles, you must re-evaluate the girth. When your horse's weight changes by more than a few pounds, you will likely need a different girth. All this means the girth is a piece of equipment we cannot take for granted. The question then becomes, "How do we choose the correct girth"?

Girth Purpose and Importance

It's evident that the purpose of the girth is to keep your saddle in place, and it seems like that shouldn't be difficult. But it depends on the horse's anatomy and movement.

In **Illustration 9.1 Anatomy of the Girth Channel Area**, you will see how the horse's elbow, being right in front of the girth channel, must be free to move back and forth. If not, there will be pinching and restriction of movement. We forget about the movement that takes place through the area of the girth channel because it is not in our line of vision. There

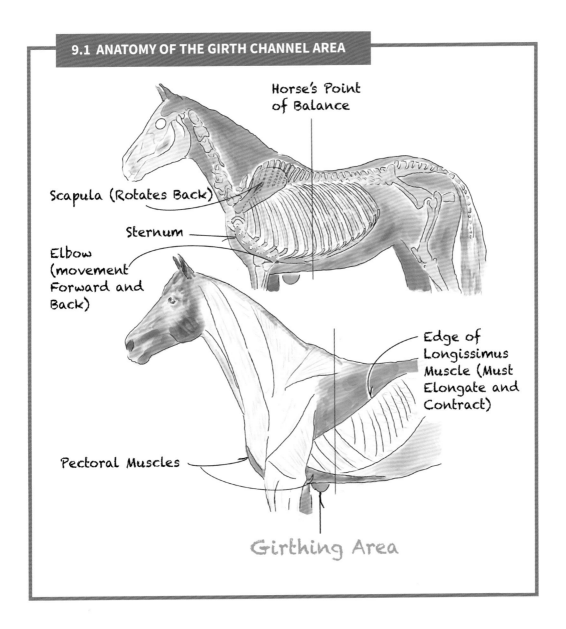

Horse's Point of Balance

Scapula (Rotates Back)

Sternum

Elbow (movement Forward and Back)

Edge of Longissimus Muscle (Must Elongate and Contract)

Pectoral Muscles

Girthing Area

is movement with each stride, each bend, each jump, each change in gait, and even each breath the horse takes. For the horse's stride to be unrestricted and regular, we also have to consider the girth. For the horse to be happy and comfortable in the work, the girth shape, length, and tightness must be right.

The horse's *elbow* area has folds of sensitive skin to allow for bending, flexing, and rotational movement. While some horses have more folds of skin than others, all horses are at risk of that skin being rubbed and pinched by the girth.

Obviously, the girth has to be tight enough to keep the saddle in place. Tightening the girth results in pressure against the *sternum*, which is out of our line of vision since it is directly underneath the horse (see **Illustration 9.1** and **Illustration 9.2 Sternum Closeup**). Because we can't easily see the sternum it is seldom considered and checked for soreness. An incorrectly shaped girth or an overly tight girth will bruise this area. This is not at all uncommon and is the reason many horses object to being girthed. The girth must *protect* the sternum. It can do this by providing a large enough surface area to distribute pressure from the girth, and ideally, by providing padding, since some horses have a sternum that is very pronounced and more at risk of bruising. Once a horse has experienced pain in the girth area, he tends to never to forget it, and you need to take extra time and care with those horses to avoid a pain response.

Long vs Short Girths

We can divide our description of girths into two general categories:

* *Long girths* for saddles with short billets. These can be pleasure, jumping, trail, dressage, and side-saddles.

* *Short girths* for saddles with long billets. These are often dressage saddles but are also found in some jumping saddles.

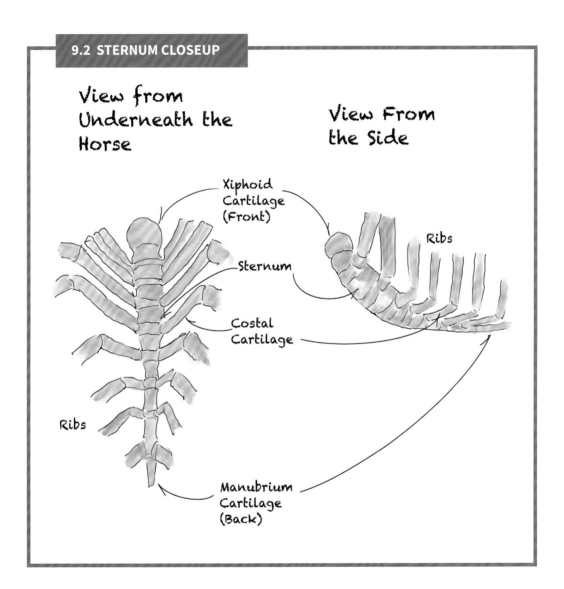

View from Underneath the Horse

View From the Side

Xiphoid Cartilage (Front)

Sternum

Costal Cartilage

Ribs

Ribs

Manubrium Cartilage (Back)

There has been a transition from long to short girths for dressage saddles, although there are still short billet dressage saddles requiring a long girth. The evolution came about as dressage riders desired a closer feel to their horses in order to make precise leg aids clearer to the horse. Riders found having girth buckles under their legs (usually around the inside of the rider's knee) to be uncomfortable and cumbersome. Two longer billets attaching the girth with buckles well below the rider's calf muscle became desirable. Subsequently, some jumper riders desired the same close feel with buckles out of the way.

Long Girth Pros and Cons

There is no doubt that a long girth is more stable on the horse because the girth attachment by the buckles is closer to the tree of the saddle (the basis of the saddle's stability). Most short billet saddles have three billets to choose from when attaching the two buckles of the girth (**Illustration 9.3 Short Billets for Long Girths**). Generally, the *first and third billet* is used because that stabilizes the front and the back of the tree. In cases where the back of the saddle tends to "float" (move too much), the *second and third billet* will be used.

Flexibility in girthing allows for greater stability of the saddle.

When the saddle tends to slip forward, the *first and second billet* will be used. For horses with withers that are not very pronounced (also termed "mutton withered"), it is very useful to have a *fourth billet,* called a *point billet,* which is more forward on the tree, and in that case that billet is attached to the girth *along with the second or middle billet.* This flexibility in girthing allows for greater stability of the saddle.

The downside of a long girth is exactly why short girths were developed, and what I've already described: there is a greater chance of discomfort in the rider from the buckles. The addition of a buckle guard at the billet area (a piece of leather that is just large enough to go over the buckles) protects the saddle leather from being damaged by the buckles but adds even more thickness under the rider's leg.

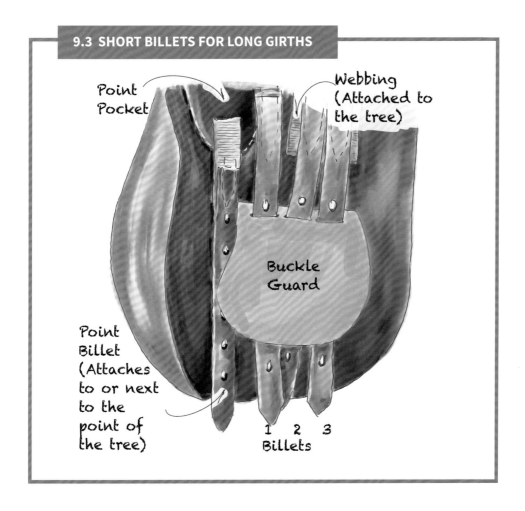

9.3 SHORT BILLETS FOR LONG GIRTHS

Point Pocket

Webbing (Attached to the tree)

Buckle Guard

Point Billet (Attaches to or next to the point of the tree)

1 2 3
Billets

Short Girth Pros and Cons

Short girths are sometimes called "dressage girths" since dressage prompted their evolution. The two long billets of a dressage saddle extend down from the tree, with the buckle of the girth located below the flap of the saddle. As already mentioned, this allows for greater freedom and comfort for the rider's leg. The long billets also have allowed for the development of a saddle that only has one piece of leather under the rider's leg: the *mono-flap* (see p. 82). The objective of the monoflap is to position the rider's leg as close to the horse as possible for reasons of both comfort and precision.

When the saddle is being secured to a girth 12 inches or so *below* where a long girth would be attached, the attachment location becomes less stationary and more ambiguous. It means the saddle shifts more readily, either front to back or side to side. *Saddle slippage* becomes the most frequent complaint regardless of whether it is caused by inexact saddle fit, rider asymmetry, or asymmetry of the horses movement. Different billeting systems have come about to help create a more secure line from the girth to the saddle tree, such as the *"V"* or *sliding billet system* (**Illustration 9.4 Long Billets for Short Girths**), where "V"-shaped webbing is used for the attachment to the back (and sometimes the front, as well) of the saddle so the location of the billet can self-adjust to the individual horse's shape. While these innovations have been helpful, they cannot make up for the instability that arises from the girth buckles being more distant from the tree.

How To Select Length Based On Fit

A *long girth* should be a length that you can easily attach on both sides of the saddle in the holes at the bottom of the billets. When tightened, the buckles should be in the middle holes of both sides.

The ideal *short girth* length is going to depend on who you talk to because for many people, aesthetics is the primary concern. Your saddle will be more stable when your buckles are within a couple of inches below the flap of your saddle. When the buckle is below the flap when tightened (allowing for some deviation due to the horse's weight fluctuations or saddle pads used) the excess billet should fit into the keeper loop on the girth and not extend so far below it that it is noticeable. Everything should be tidy and contained.

Tightened in either a long girth or a short girth means the saddle is secure but you can insert your fingertips between the girth and the horse. This is an advantage of a girth with

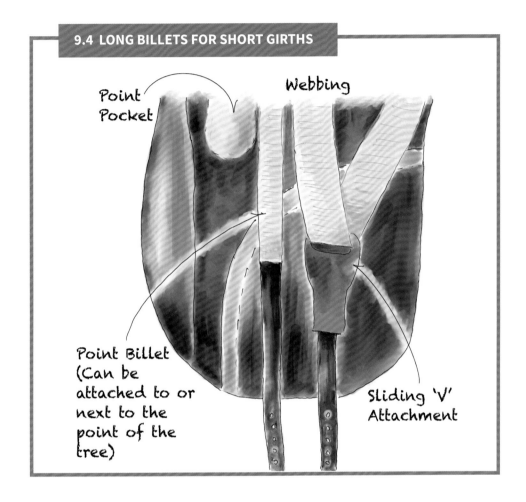

Point Pocket

Webbing

Point Billet (Can be attached to or next to the point of the tree)

Sliding 'V' Attachment

elastic, which is nice to have on both sides of the girth as it keeps the pressure more even. Notice in **Illustration 9.5 Girth Tightness** the anatomically shaped girth that has been adjusted in a fashion that is not overly tight. Remember that overly tight girths restrict the horse's ability to move, bend, and breathe. Examine a prospective girth carefully since there are some designs that may or may not be to your horse's benefit in terms of comfort and performance.

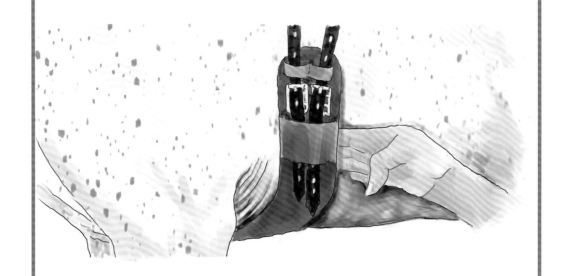

Should easily be able to insert fingertips under Girth but should be snug.

Notice Girth placement gives room behind elbow and skin wrinkles, padding under buckles, billets can be adjusted at different holes depending on horse shape.

Shapes of Girths (and Buckle Types)

There are basic shapes for long or short girths (**Illustration 9.6 Shapes of Long Girths** and **Illustration 9.7 Shapes of Short Girths**). These shapes are recent developments as equestrians require girths that take into account the variety of horse shapes we are trying to fit, the increasing athleticism of the breeds, and our increasing understanding of how horses

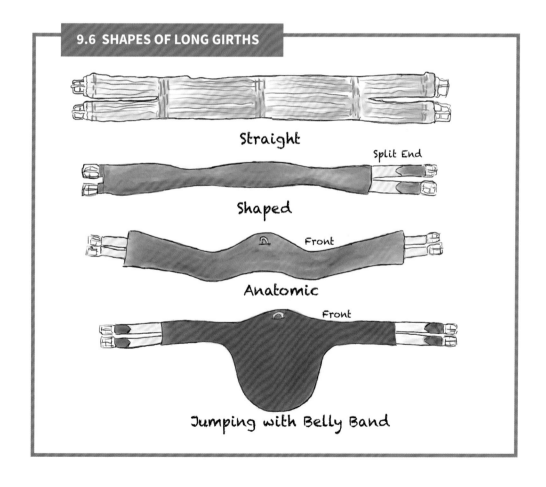

9.6 SHAPES OF LONG GIRTHS

Straight

Shaped — Split End

Anatomic — Front

Jumping with Belly Band — Front

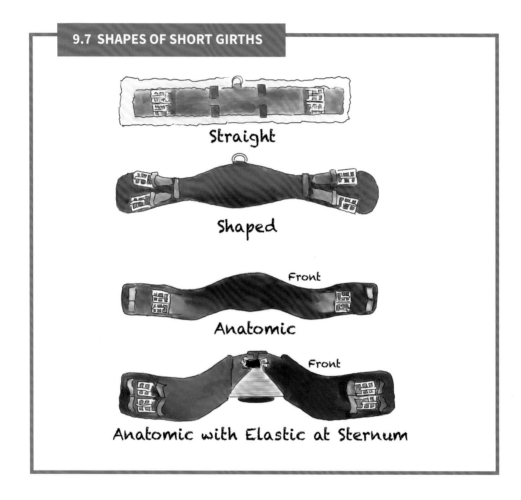

Straight

Shaped

Front

Anatomic

Front

Anatomic with Elastic at Sternum

are impacted by having the correct size and shape of girth. What are the advantages and disadvantages of the basic shapes?

✳ **Straight girths** are basically rectangles with buckles at each end. Usually made of leather, but sometimes of cloth or string, they are the most economical to produce. They do not account for the room needed at the horse's elbow and can cause rubbing and sores. They do not provide additional surface area at the sternum and can cause undue pressure directly underneath the horse. They are, however, versatile and will work on many horse shapes, and in the case of string girths, which allow the shape to conform more readily to the horse's unique features, they can be a good choice.

* **Shaped girths** are tapered like a double hourglass, becoming narrower at the elbow area and wider at the sternum. They are customarily padded and rolled on the edges to reduce the chance of rubbing. These girths work well for horses with uncomplicated conformation and are useful for horses with narrow girth channels. Because they work well on a number of horses, they are a good choice for stables that use a particular girth on multiple horses.

Shaped girths can fit well on a number of different types of horses.

* **Anatomical girths** take into account the many cases where the billets of the saddle, whether long or short, fall behind the girth channel. Horses that have a long, sloping shoulder will require saddle placement well behind the scapula to allow for that horse's unrestricted movement, resulting in billets that fall over the swell of the rib cage, behind the girth channel. If a straight or shaped girth is used on these horses, the girth will pull the saddle forward. An anatomical girth curves forward to go into the girth channel and fall over the sternum. Note that these girths are *not* symmetrical and it is possible to place them on the horse backward. (**Illustrations 9.6 Shapes of Long Girths and 9.7 Shapes of Short Girths** show the front and back placement.)

* **Jumping girths** are much wider and much more padded at the sternum, mainly to protect the horse from his metal shoes, often with studs or cleats for traction, when he folds his knees to clear a jump. Horses run the risk of painful bruising and cuts without these protective girths (see **Illustrations 9.6 and 9.8 Long Girth Placement on Horse**).

Placement of the Girth

Commonly, the front of the girth on an English saddle should be a hands' width behind the elbow of the horse. This allows for movement of the elbow as well as folds of skin at the elbow. In most cases, this placement keeps the girth in the girth channel. However, when the girth is in the girth channel but the back of the girth lies over the swell of the rib cage, the horse has a *narrow girth channel*. The solution is not to bring the girth more forward since that will pull the saddle into the incorrect position, blocking the scapula, but instead to use a girth that is shaped or anatomical and narrow enough at the area behind the elbows. This is where you need to try different shapes to find one that will work for your horse. (**Note**: there is *no* consistency in measurement of girths and while a certain "size" might work well from one manufacturer, the same size from a different brand may be too short or too long.)

To visualize correct placement of a girth, see **Illustration 9.8 Long Girth Placement on Horse** and **Illustration 9.9 Short Girth Placement on Horse**.

Girth Parts and Materials—Pros and Cons

The options for girth materials are extensive, but most fall within the basics listed here:

✳ **Leather girths** are the most common material used because of the durability and malleability of leather. They can be easily cleaned, oiled or conditioned, and repaired, and they will last a very long time if cared for. The type of leather used is usually cowhide, which is not going to stretch easily and is often treated to withstand sweat. The cost is quite variable, depending on the quality of materials and the manufacturer.

✳ **Synthetic girths** are often less expensive and available as in both straight and shaped options. Rarely are they available in an anatomical shape. There are some specialty

Showing shaped saddle pad contouring the shape of the saddle.

Jumping Girth with belly guard. Note shape for the elbow allows for movement.

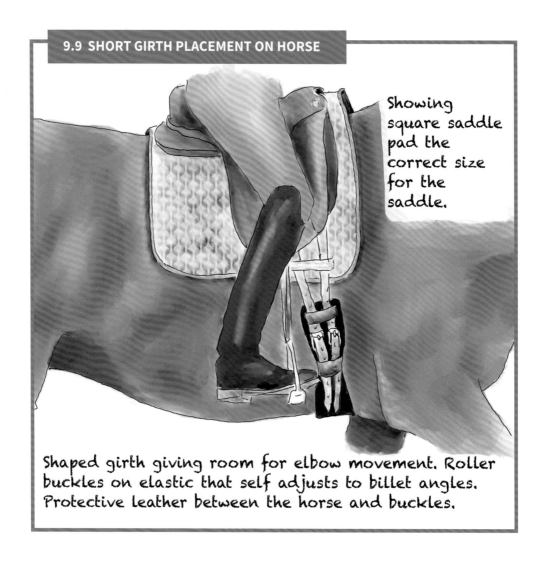

9.9 SHORT GIRTH PLACEMENT ON HORSE

Showing square saddle pad the correct size for the saddle.

Shaped girth giving room for elbow movement. Roller buckles on elastic that self adjusts to billet angles. Protective leather between the horse and buckles.

synthetic girths that, even if they are straight in shape, were developed to avoid chafing by virtue of their flexibility and texture. These clean very easily with just water.

✳ **Cloth and string girths** have been around for a very long time. They are predominantly straight in shape but conform to the horse's shape nicely because of the virtues of their material. Horses with very narrow girth channels typically do well with string girths. The term "string" is used even though the material is actually cord. The cord or cloth was traditionally cotton although synthetic blends, and sometimes wool blends, are now also offered. These girths are economical and long-wearing. They generally do not come with elastic ends because of the inherent elasticity of the fabric or cording. They are easily cleaned in a bucket of water.

❋ **Sheepskin** is technically leather but falls into a different category of girth material because the fleece is generally stabilized by stitching it to leather or nylon. Natural sheepskin breathes well, easily conforms to the shape of the horse, and never chafes if it is clean and soft. It does allow for some slippage, however. It is also more costly and requires special soap and care or the sheepskin will get dry and stiff. Synthetic sheepskin is available, which is less expensive and easier to care for, but it slips very easily and can create heat buildup (it doesn't behave with the qualities of natural sheepskin).

❋ **Elastic ends** at the buckles of the girth is a distinct advantage. It makes girthing easier and allows some "give" as your horse moves and breathes. Elastic should be either double or triple thickness. The type of elastic used is specifically designed for girths with less elasticity and greater durability than what you would commonly see in the clothing industry.

❋ **Buckles** are a very important part of the girth. Never use a girth without *roller buckles* as shown in **Illustration 9.10 Girth Buckle**. Roller buckles have a tube or roller around the top of the buckle so that your billet will not get chewed up every time you use it. Not only will girthing be smoother and easier for you, you won't have the repair costs from frequently replacing damaged billets. Make sure the tongue of the buckle (the part that goes through the hole of the billet) is smooth and not jagged. Rough spots on the tongue of the buckle will make gashes in the underside of the leather of your saddle flap. There are *spring buckles*, usually found on synthetic girths, which are supposed to make girthing easier when mounted. They are notorious for gouging the underside of billets. Damage to billets is a serious safety threat. If one of your billets breaks while you are riding, the saddle can

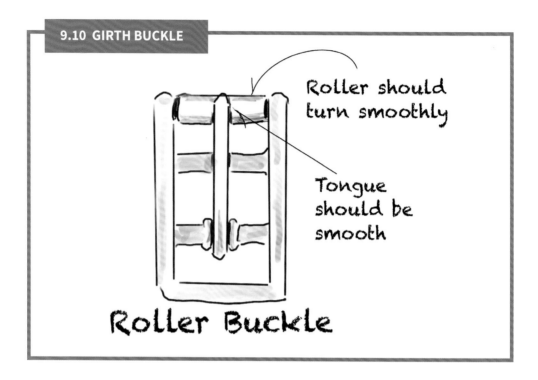

Roller should turn smoothly

Tongue should be smooth

Roller Buckle

suddenly go crooked on the horse, which is alarming to both horse and rider. (And we know what will happen if both billets break!)

Care, Maintenance, and Safety

The girth is going to be exposed to more dirt and sweat than your saddle so it should be cleaned *every time* you use it. The way you clean it is going to depend on the girth's material (see p. 123). Dirty girths cause girth sores. Girth sores are *very* hard to get rid of, and you will not be riding your horse when he has them. The time it takes to clean and condition your girth is very worthwhile. Leaving a dirty girth lying over the top of a saddle for more than a few minutes will damage the seat leather of your saddle. Horse sweat is corrosive and will pull oils out of the seat leather, causing it to dry and crack. (See more on care of tack in chapter 11, p. 136).

Saddle Pads

Are saddle pads:

* Simply a way to keep your saddle clean?

* A remedy for a saddle fit problem?

* A therapy for a horse with back or skin issues?

* A fashion statement?

* Brand recognition for a barn, trainer, or saddlery?

The answer is different for every horse-and-rider combination. It helps to have perspective when analyzing the entire saddle fit scenario, and ask yourself the question, "Why am I using *this* pad?" Using pads differs from country to country. In the United Kingdom, for example, you may not use a saddle pad (*numnah*) at all. I found that barns that put great importance on maintaining saddle fit found they could determine much more about how saddles were fitting when they were placed directly on the horse's back. When riding in Iceland, a rubber-like, rectangular pad that draped over the horse's back was the only thing used under the saddle. It was breathable with holes, gave a layer of compression over the back, protected the withers, perfectly conformed to the horse's back, did not allow the saddle to slip, and could be rinsed off after every use. In this case as well, saddle fit was constantly monitored.

It is interesting that when riding in areas that are *market driven*, where there are high numbers of equestrian product consumers, we see many different types of saddle pads. It's not uncommon to notice in the United States, especially at horse show venues, a saddle being used with *multiple* pads. It is probably not coincidental that these are areas where saddle fit maintenance is less emphasized, considerably misunderstood, or generally unavailable. Where there are fewer skilled certified saddlers to maintain proper saddle fit, there are more retailers to sell alternatives to fit in the way of saddle pads.

Basic Saddle Pad Shapes

Practically speaking, the English style saddle pad is used to:

* Keep the saddle clean from sweat and dirt from the horse's back.

* Absorb sweat, thus protecting the panel of the saddle from corrosive sweat.

* Provide a bit of cushioning for the horse's back under the saddle.

The saddle pad is *not* intended to:

* Be a substitute for correct saddle fit.

* Be a remedy for putting a saddle on multiple horses without scrutiny.

The shape of English saddle pads is intended to complement the shape and size of the saddle in two basic categories: *shaped* and *square.*

Shaped pads (see **Illustration 9.8,** p. 121) should follow the outside dimensions of the saddle. When the saddle is a dressage saddle, the shape of the pad will have a long, straight front edge and will match the length of the flap with about an inch of the pad extending beyond the saddle in all directions. If the pad is too small, whether in width or length, it will cause a pressure point under the saddle. If it is too large it will be more likely for the pad to shift and move under the saddle. It also looks aesthetically messy to have too much pad extending from the saddle area.

Square pads (see **Illustration 9.9**, p. 122) are a rectangular shape that should be slightly larger than the saddle in length and width. The square shape makes it possible to pin an entry number to the pad behind the rider's leg at horse shows. While there is some room for artistic license in the shape of the pad (for example, it may have a *swallowtail corner* or a *curved corner*) the shape is still considered "square."

For *any* saddle pad, it is important that the shape of the pad allows space for the horse's withers as in **Illustration 10.1 Laminated Grip Pad**. Some saddle pads are straight across where they cross over the spine and do not have the necessary curve to accommodate the bony protrusion of the withers. Even if the horse does not have high withers when standing still, it is important to allow room for the withers to rise when he is in motion. Saddle pads should be pulled up, front to back, into the gullet of the saddle before the saddle is secured with the girth. Remember how important it was to protect the horse's spinous processes with the gullet of the saddle. It is the same with the saddle pad: if it presses down on the spine, you are causing a problem.

Ideally, there are fabric loops sewn onto the saddle pad which the billets and girth will pass through to keep things secure. Sometimes they are not placed correctly for a saddle, in which case, have them altered so they match your billet placement.

Pad Material

Some of the common materials used for saddle pads are:

* **100 percent cotton**, generally in a twill or weave and heavy enough to withstand wear. I've never known a horse that had a problem with cotton as it is very absorbent and

10.1 LAMINATED GRIP PAD

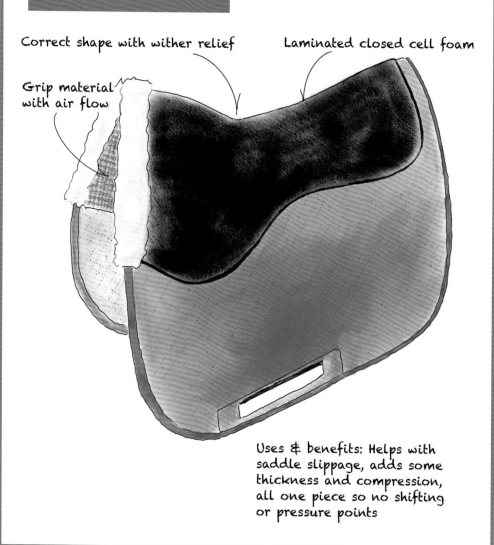

Correct shape with wither relief

Laminated closed cell foam

Grip material with air flow

Uses & benefits: Helps with saddle slippage, adds some thickness and compression, all one piece so no shifting or pressure points stays in place. However, if the shape is not correct, it will rub and abrade the horse's hair and skin. Cotton launders well but will fade over time.

* **Cotton/synthetic blends** wear well, they don't fade as easily, they are economical, and they dry more quickly than 100 percent cotton. They are usually more slick and can move under the saddle on some horses. Some horses do not tolerate synthetic fabrics well and can develop skin bumps.

* **Synthetic fabrics** can be appealing because of color choices and cost but can be quite slippery. They often do not stay in place. This is also true of synthetic fleece. Again, some horses do not tolerate synthetic fabrics well.

* **Natural sheepskin** pads, as long as they are clean and soft, conform nicely to the shape of the horse, breathe well, are very absorbent, and last a long time if cared for correctly. They can cause a saddle to slip more easily, however.

* **Wool fabric** is infrequently used in woven pads because of the care required to clean it, but wool blends are available that are very absorbent and stay in place.

The thickness, lining, and quilting are additional material-related issues to consider when using a saddle pad.

* The *thin pads with open cell foam* (such as *foam rubber*) used in the quilting don't offer cushioning to the horse because they compress easily. These types of pads are also not very absorbent so the bottom of your saddle will become sweaty.

* *Thicker quilted pads*, usually with a *cotton blend fill*, are highly absorbent and breathable, giving the horse more cushioning.

Care of most saddle pads will be related to their material and stated on their label, but most are designed to be laundered in a washing machine. Take care that the washing machine is large enough for the pad and that a gentle or hand wash option is used. Do not use an excessive amount of laundry soap, and keep in mind soap without additives reduces your chances of your horse having an allergic reaction since it is difficult to get all the soap rinsed from a saddle pad. Never place a saddle pad in a dryer. Always line dry it.

Therapeutic Pads

The options for *therapeutic pads* are being offered at an increasing rate as our understanding of equine back health evolves and access to specialized materials becomes available. There is a carryover from materials used for hospitals and human health care and access to materials tested for maximum shock absorbency. There is also renewed appreciation for natural fibers that can be used in new ways. Rather than filling your tack room with pads and draining your bank account, thinking through the process in a way that complements correct saddle fitting, rather than tries to substitute for it, will give you the tools to ensure your horse's health and comfort.

Here are a few sample scenarios when I have recommended therapeutic pads:

✳ There are many cases when horses lose weight or topline and are expected to eventually gain it back. Losing conditioning can happen very quickly, or it can be a slow process that can take you by surprise when you go to do your regular saddle evaluation and find that your saddle is suddenly too close to your horse's spine. In cases where only a small amount of additional thickness is needed, an ideal solution is a single thicker saddle pad or a laminated grip pad (see **Illustration 10.1,** p. 128). When more thickness is needed, adding a pad between your cloth saddle pad and your saddle will give your saddle the temporary lift you need until that muscle returns. There are various thicknesses and materials but here are things to consider:

- Add only the thickness that you need to provide the required room for the spine. *More is not better*—it makes your saddle unstable.

- Make sure that the material you use is the thickness you need when it is *under compression.* Do the *pinch test.* When you squeeze the material, it should "give" no more than 20 percent. Think about the fact that your saddle is carrying the weight of the rider, and think about the force of the horse moving upward plus the force of the rider coming down into the saddle with movement.

- In general, *open cell foam*, commonly called *foam rubber,* is not going to do much to keep the saddle up off the spine. *Closed cell foam*, which traps the air inside the space of the pad, is a preferable material. *Felted material* also works wonderfully! It compresses little but forms well over the shape of the horse's back.

✳ For the rider with more than one horse, she may find that one saddle fits one horse well. The fit on a different horse might be very close but perhaps that horse is slightly less wide or has less topline. For this situation, consider a *compression pad* (**Illustration 10.2 Compression Pad**) for the horse that has less topline. Maybe the issue is the second horse is balanced more uphill or downhill. Adding a *balance pad* (**Illustration 10.3 Balance Pad**) may make the correction that you need. Because these are seamless pads with wither relief, placing them between the saddle and your regular saddle pad avoids pressure points *as long as the therapeutic pad is the correct length for your saddle*. It is important in these cases to fit the saddle to the widest horse. Then, using the therapeutic pad, address the check points of good saddle fit discussed in this book to make sure the padding arrangement is correcting the fit. Not everyone can have a saddle for each horse they ride, but everyone *can* evaluate the saddle on each horse to assure correct fit.

✳ As we have discussed, asymmetry in horses' backs is common, and many times it is necessary to use a therapeutic or balance pad to keep the saddle straight on the horse while

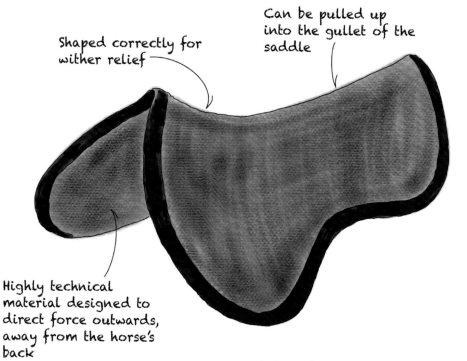

Can be pulled up into the gullet of the saddle

Shaped correctly for wither relief

Highly technical material designed to direct force outwards, away from the horse's back

Uses & benefits: Designed to provide room for the horse's spine, reduces force on the horse's back, different sizes & shapes to accommodate different saddles, easy to care for, durable

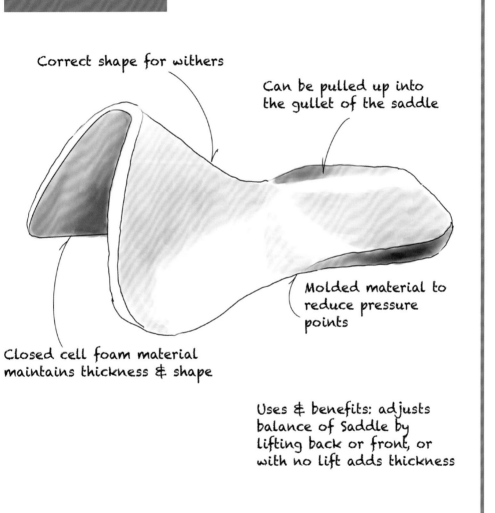

Correct shape for withers

Can be pulled up into
the gullet of the saddle

Molded material to
reduce pressure
points

Closed cell foam material
maintains thickness & shape

Uses & benefits: adjusts
balance of saddle by
lifting back or front, or
with no lift adds thickness

you use exercises under saddle, address hoof care, or use other rehabilitation methods to bring the horse's body into balance. Some horses remain asymmetrical, but in either case—temporary or chronic—we must keep the saddle symmetrical and address the fit through balance pads or *shim pads* (**Illustration 10.4 Shim Half Pad**). For example, a horse that is less developed on the right side will need shims on the right side. A horse that has a diagonal asymmetry, such as less developed behind the right shoulder (less right *trapezius* muscle) and less muscle over the left back (less left *longissimus dorsi* muscle) will require a shim or balance pad in the right front and the left rear (see **Illustration 3.9,** p. 22).

✳ *Saddle slip* is a very common problem for many different issues. The cause of saddle slippage is not always incorrect saddle fit. In many cases, the way the horse moves causes the saddle to slip forward or to the side. Subtle lameness is a frequent cause of the saddle consistently slipping to one side, as is rider asymmetry. After carefully making sure the saddle meets all the proper fit requirements, non-slip saddle pads can be very helpful (see **Illustration 10.2**). These pads are grippy on the *horse side* (bottom) of the pad and on the *saddle side* (top). There are also thin grippy pads available that can be inserted between the saddle and the saddle pad. These pads generally have special cleaning instructions that must be followed, and the pads *must* be clean in order to be effective.

✳ A horse with a dropped or sway back will need a therapeutic pad, in most cases. Not all horses that have a dropped back are aged horses—some situations are congenital or caused from the horse being ridden at too early an age. The backs of these horses are not always in pain, but they are weaker and more at risk of spinal damage. I have made custom pads for horses like this, but with manufactured shim pads now available, it is not difficult to add shims where needed to adjust the saddle to the horse. Keep in mind you still have to keep the gullet of the saddle open to make sure there is no pressure over the spinous process.

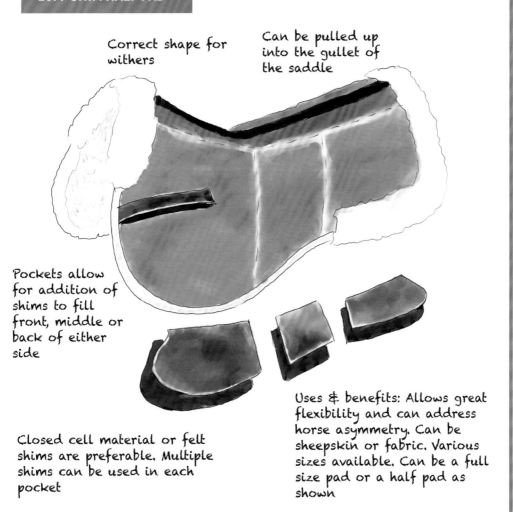

Correct shape for withers

Can be pulled up into the gullet of the saddle

Pockets allow for addition of shims to fill front, middle or back of either side

Closed cell material or felt shims are preferable. Multiple shims can be used in each pocket

Uses & benefits: Allows great flexibility and can address horse asymmetry. Can be sheepskin or fabric. Various sizes available. Can be a full size pad or a half pad as shown

11 Repairs, Maintenance, and Resources

The best strategy for purchasing and maintaining your tack is:

✳ Buy the best you can afford. The "best" may not be the most expensive.

✳ Understand how to choose the best saddle fit option for your horse and regularly re-evaluate. Make a schedule to check your saddle fit and saddle safety either by yourself or through an experienced saddle fitter.

✳ Have a maintenance schedule to clean and condition your tack (**Illustration 11.1 Cleaning and Conditioning**):

• Clean your tack after every ride if possible. If not, once a week cleaning followed by conditioning the leather.

• Girths definitely need to be cleaned after every ride because of the sensitivity of skin in the girth channel. Condition girths at least once per week as dry leather will abrade the skin.

• Saddle pads need to be washed or hosed off to keep them clean. When your saddle pad is extremely sweaty or dirty after a ride, it needs to be washed afterward. Sometimes weekly washing is sufficient.

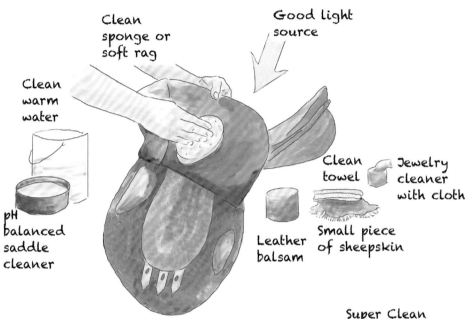

Clean sponge or soft rag

Good light source

Clean warm water

pH balanced saddle cleaner

Clean towel

Jewelry cleaner with cloth

Leather balsam

Small piece of sheepskin

After your ride:
* Place your saddle on a saddle rack or smooth table under a good light source
* Use a sponge with cleaner to clean All surfaces on BOTH sides, rinsing often, minimizing water
* Wipe dry with clean towel

Once per week ALSO:
* After thoroughly cleaning and drying
*In a warm area
*Use your hands to apply leather balsam letting the heat of your hands and the friction of rubbing onto all surfaces cause the balsam to soak in
* Rub off remaining balsam with sheepskin

Super Clean Monthly ALSO:
* After thoroughly cleaning and conditioning
* Use a jewelry cleaning cloth or metal "wadding" to clean: stirrup bars and other hardware taking care to avoid touching leather

- When cleaning your saddle, remove the stirrup leathers. Swap them when you reattach them so that one doesn't become longer than the other. Even leathers that are reinforced with nylon will stretch enough to make the rider uneven.

- Use careful cleaning and conditioning as a way to check for damage or excessive wear of your tack. Noticing things early will avoid accidents.

- Keep your saddle on a thick blanket or cushion over a saddle rack to avoid deforming the panels.

- Keep your saddle covered with a non-abrasive saddle cover. Put a waterproof cover or sheet over it if you have it in a barn that could leak.

- A temperature-controlled tack room is preferable for tack storage but not always possible. It is best to avoid excessive cold or heat as it is hard on the leather.

- When possible, keep your tack room locked. Theft happens. Stolen saddles are increasing in number. Keep a file with the manufacturer's name, saddle's model, size for the horse, size for the rider, and serial number. Also, the receipt or show the date purchased and amount paid. If possible, list this in your homeowner's or renter's insurance policy. Photographs of the saddle are useful to include in the file.

✳ Be familiar with how to best care for and maintain your equipment with the correct care products. Consult the manufacturer for recommended products.

- Leather cleaner should be pH-balanced and recommended for English tack, which primarily uses vegetable tanned leather (Western tack is generally oak tanned leather so is treated differently). Using a plain damp cloth or sponge cleaned constantly with warm water is preferable to using the incorrect product. Do not use excessive water.

- Leather conditioner should be used regularly. If your saddle is used daily, pick one day a week to thoroughly clean it, followed by conditioning. Do *not* oil or condition leather that has not be cleaned first since that just seals the dirt and sweat into your leather. Products with beeswax seal the oils in the leather for a longer time and are helpful in arid regions.

✳ When you find a repair issue, address it promptly before it becomes worse.

Storage Concerns

As a final note related to safety, store saddles individually on a saddle rack or something comparable. They should *never* be stacked on top of each other for a few reasons:

✳ Stacked saddles tend to be unstable, and if knocked over could incur damage.

✳ Stacking can deform the saddle panels (the panel of the saddle above can be dented when sitting against the cantle of the saddle underneath).

  Here are some saddler tips for keeping your saddle in optimal condition:

- Place a saddle cover or a blanket on each saddle. This should be waterproof if you are concerned about a leaky room (or cats).

- When storing a saddle on a saddle rack, place a thick blanket on the rack underneath the saddle so that the rack doesn't deform the underside of your saddle.

- When transporting the saddle in your car, place it either upside down on top of a blanket or propped up on the pommel, resting against a non-abrasive surface. Do not leave your saddle for prolonged periods in a hot car.

- When setting your saddle on the ground for short periods of time, place it on the pommel against a non-abrasive surface.

Repairs and Maintenance

Repairs and maintenance support are highly variable depending on your location. England and France, for example, have a high population of *qualified saddle fitters* (educated to fit English-style saddles) and *qualified saddlers* (educated to make and repair saddles) to choose from. That selection generally means you will have a higher quality of skilled

Make sure a saddler is qualified before hiring him to work on your saddle.

professionals because of professional competition. If you are from my state of Colorado in the United States, your options are considerably more limited. While some say they are saddlers or saddle fitters, many are self-taught and self-professed in their field, and the results of their work should be reviewed prior to committing to hiring them. Individuals who have been trained and certified by a legitimate saddlery institution are committed to a standard of work established by that institution. This is a long way of saying, *do your research before engaging a saddler to work on your saddle.*

To find a qualified saddler for repairs, the internet is your friend. You may hear of referrals from your friends at the barn or trainers but *always* do your homework yourself. Look them up. They will probably have websites where they state their backgrounds and credentials. A handy resource is the Society of Master Saddlers UK (SMS) website where they list saddlers and fitters by geographic location. To be a member of this group, the individuals must be trained, tested, and certified; they must address any grievances through the SMS protocol; they must keep up their continuing education; and they must pay yearly fees. There are other institutions that promote the trade, and it is important that you are familiar with their standards. You will often find that certified and trained individuals are *not* more expensive but offer a much better service. Having worked with or for a qualified fitter does *not* make an individual qualified but may assist with that individual's training.

Common repairs such as replacing billets, stitching repairs, rebalancing a panel, or a strip/reflock of a panel should be relatively easy to accomplish, although you may need to ship your saddle to a qualified shop. If a saddler works on Western saddles, do *not* assume that they know how to work on English saddles! English saddlers doing modifications and repairs have been trained for this specialty. We have different tools that are designed for these particular saddles (**Illustration 11.2 Saddlery Tools** shows a few that I regularly use).

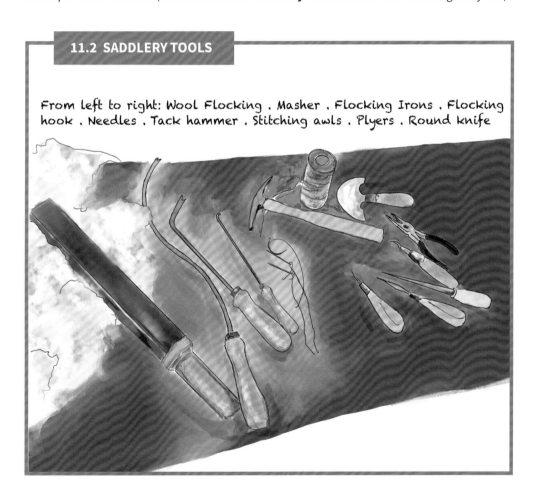

11.2 SADDLERY TOOLS

From left to right: Wool Flocking . Masher . Flocking Irons . Flocking hook . Needles . Tack hammer . Stitching awls . Plyers . Round knife

Most of the stitching is done by hand, not by machine. This requires skill and technique (along with strong hands and good lighting). Check the prices before shipping! Make sure that the work is guaranteed and get that in writing through an email or message. Find out what happens if you need follow-up work. And when you are happy with the work and happy with the business relationship, make sure to let the saddler know you appreciate their work, give good reviews, and stay in touch. As long as you have tack, it will always need maintenance and repair.

With the use of this book, horse owners, riders, and trainers can develop a good idea of what is right, what is wrong, and what the next steps should be when it comes to proper saddle fit. The more you put these skills to use, the more the process will make sense and the better you will be at analysis. Understanding and appreciating these skills will create a better life for your horses. Your horses will certainly thank you!

And thank *you* for your quest for knowledge, for opening your mind to a different perspective, and for being part of a caring horse community!

Acknowledgments

There are so many who I wish to thank for their teachings, their support, and their confidence in this artistic writing endeavor.

My husband Brad has been an integral part of this collection of knowledge and shares bottomless love of the horses.

My friend and teacher Keith Bryan has my deepest respect and gratitude for welcoming me into his saddlery business as well as his home in the United Kingdom.

To my current saddle fitting apprentice Jimmy Nedeljkovic, this book benefitted from your input, and I have learned much from you. Ours has been the ideal mentor/apprenticeship relationship.

My decades-long relationship with the Society of Master Saddlers UK has been most directly with Hazel Morley, who to my eyes, runs the show. Your support and your constant efforts have resulted in the spread of valuable knowledge that is necessary to help the horses and riders we serve. Thank you for including me in your program—the best of the best.

For many years, I have been in awe of the knowledge and skill of Nancy Loving, DVM, who added her touch to the making of this book and had confidence in its completion.

It is through continuing education that I have taken a number of classes from Dr. Russell MacKechnie-Guire, Centaur Biomechanics. I am so appreciative of the continual accessibility of new knowledge through his programs, which are presented by the best professionals worldwide for the good of the horses. By keeping knowledge fresh and accessible, the most current information feeds the equestrian community.

If it were not for the insight and skill of the staff of Trafalgar Square, this book may not have come to fruition. My appreciation for all you have done to create and distribute this book will continue through time.

Index